THE EFFECT OF ADVERTISING AND DISPLAY

Assessing the Evidence

THE EFFECT OF ADVERTISING AND DISPLAY

Assessing the Evidence

Robert East
Kingston Business School

KLUWER ACADEMIC PUBLISHERS
Boston / Dordrecht / New York / London

Distributors for North, Central and South America:
Kluwer Academic Publishers
101 Philip Drive
Assinippi Park
Norwell, Massachusetts 02061 USA
Telephone (781) 871-6600
Fax (781) 681-9045
E-Mail <kluwer@wkap.com>
Distributors for all other countries:
Kluwer Academic Publishers Group
Post Office Box 17
3300 AH Dordrecht, THE NETHERLANDS
Tel: +31 (0) 78 657 60 00
Fax: +31 (0) 78 657 64 74

E-Mail <services@wkap.nl>

 Electronic Services <http://www.wkap.nl>

East, Robert.
    The effect of advertising and display: assessing the evidence
        p.cm.
    Includes bibliographical references and index.
ISBN 1-4020-7514-6

The Publisher offers discounts on this book for course use and bulk purchases.
For further information, send email to <kluwer@wkap.com>.

Contents

List of Figures

List of Tables

Preface

Why?

Advertising is arguably the most interesting of all the business fields. It requires a range of human skills that are both creative and practical and, when successful, can have a strong effect on business performance. How does advertising work? Despite its importance, this question gets limited attention in many textbooks on marketing communications. Such books address the goals and methods of agencies and their clients, the practice of copywriting, integrated marketing communications, the choice of media, advertising cases, business and legal constraints etc, but the evidence for the effects of advertising and the processes involved in producing these effects are usually given little space.

This is a pity. Explaining how advertising works is difficult but both students and practitioners want to know about the methods of research, the debates and uncertainties, and the more solid conclusions now available about the effects of advertising. And we certainly have some findings to report. There has been a steady stream of research from both academics and practitioners and much of this work is relevant to business practice.

What?

This book cannot be comprehensive and is not intended to be. Rather, it addresses the *gaps* in the treatments of conventional texts. First, I have tried to cover both the academic and practitioner work that is relevant; too often, one is ignored by exponents of the other. This means that, in addition to conventional academic sources, I have used papers from *Admap* and cases from the *Advertising Works* series in the UK and *Effective Advertising* in Australia. Second, I have given detailed consideration to the psychological mechanisms that may explain observed ad effects. Third, I have addressed the long-term sales effects of advertising, which may be even stronger than the primary effects. Here, I have given particular attention to the social processes that are involved. Fourth, I have examined the way in which behavior may be affected at the point of purchase since it is here that the effects of media advertising may be reawakened. There is evidence of strong effects on sales from point-of-sale material and we need to understand how these effects may come about. Fifth, I have tried to cover important recent developments, including the ways in which online advertising can work.

This book does not provide a full discussion of media effects; TV advertising is emphasized because of the good research in this field and Internet advertising is examined because of the interest in this new medium. Also, the treatment of segmentation issues is limited to those based on loyalty, weight of television viewing, and weight of brand purchase.

Advertising uses many different types of appeal and a range of media to achieve a variety of goals. Different ads for the same brand can have markedly different effects and the same ad can produce different effects in different audience segments. This seems a recipe for chaos but, as our knowledge has expanded, a more coherent account of the consumer response to advertising has emerged. I have tried to map out what we know, but I also indicate the uncertainties that remain and suggest what may apply when we lack good evidence. I hope that the difference between claims based on evidence and suggestions based on judgment is clear in the text.

Who For?

This book is relevant to two groups. In the business community, it should help users and practitioners of advertising who seek a more research-based understanding of the subject. In the academic community, it should meet the needs of more advanced students (first-degree specialists and post-graduates). Over the years, I have taught a large number of such people. I have been impressed by their skill and their quest for greater knowledge and this book is written with them in mind.

Plan of the Book

- Chapter 1 is concerned with the nature of effective advertising and shows how ads may increase sales, raise margins and improve business efficiency.

- Chapter 2 examines how sales relate to the number and concentration of ad exposures and to the implications of this evidence for the scheduling of ads. In this Chapter we look at theories about how a number of ad exposures may act together.

- Chapter 3 extends the evidence on ad outcomes by assessing how the effect of a particular ad wears out with repeated exposure and how any ad effect that has been established in the audience decays over time. A model of how ads work is introduced. In this model, ads act via two routes, primary and carryover. The primary route changes behavior either by thoughtful processes or by automatic mechanisms. The carryover route is longer term and produces behavioral effects as a result of persisting changes in the buyer's thinking, learning from purchase, distribution changes, and social influence. In this Chapter, we also look at the levels of response to advertising shown by different audience segments.

- Chapter 4 is concerned with more detailed explanations of the role of reflective processes and automatic mechanisms in inducing behavioral change. We examine the conditions that secure attention and look at the evidence on the mechanisms that may be used to process advertising.

- Chapter 5 deals with the interplay between ad content and purchase context. Many sales take place in a different time and place from the advertising. This focuses attention on the trace that is left in individuals by media advertising and its reactivation at the point of purchase. Some advertising will be more effective under specific purchase conditions, and we try to show how product, message and media can be matched to advantage. The joint effect of price, display and local advertising are briefly reviewed.

- Chapter 6 deals briefly with issues raised by online advertising, particularly its direct and indirect effects and the means used to serve ads that are related to the interests of the recipients.

- In a short Postscript, some applications of this work are highlighted.

Acknowledgements

In writing this book, I have received substantial help from colleagues who read draft versions. The book is much the better for their contributions. In particular, I am indebted to: Gianluigi Guido, Kathy Hammond, Janet Hoek, Rachel Kennedy, Wendy Lomax, Colin McDonald, Andrew Roberts, John Rossiter, John Scriven, Mark Uncles, and Gill Willson.

I have used findings from work conducted by past students, particularly on word-of-mouth effects. My thanks go to: Buddhika Arandara, Elizabeth Torres Bardales, Silvia Ceballos, Michelle Clark, Davison Cunjamalay, Valeria David, Maria Francolini, Edward Freeman, William Gilsenan, Caitlin Gomes, Caroline Hancock, Christopher Holloway, Stephanie Mabey, David Mackie, Radhika Narain, Lucinda Pearce, Jayne Pedder, Jane Riddle, Rakhi Solanki, Jason Veerapatrapillay, and Michael Williamson.

I also acknowledge the help of Trevor Beattie (TBWA, UK), Tim Broadbent (Bates), Reg Bryson (The Campaign Palace, Australia), Jordan Louviere, (UTS, Australia), Iain Moir (Health Development Agency, UK) Hamish Pringle (Institute of Practitioners in Advertising, UK), Marco Rimini (JWT), Jeffrey Wallis, and Terry Williams.

I would like to record my debt to Simon Broadbent who died in 2002. He was a tireless researcher and a great supporter of others who struggled to explain ad effects. This book, with its many references to Simon's work, reflects the enormous contribution that he made in this field.

Chapter 1
WHAT IS EFFECTIVE ADVERTISING?

*What must be influenced if ads are to be effective? Ultimately, this is behavior. The behavior that most people focus on is **buying** but this has two aspects: buying **more** and buying at **higher prices**. In addition, advertising can affect the operations of a company so that internal efficiencies are made and **costs** are reduced.*

Ads succeed by affecting behavior. In social contexts, ads may reduce accidents, increase voting rates, encourage passengers to wear seatbelts, promote healthy eating, and help people to stop smoking. In the commercial setting, advertising works on activities such as purchasing, renting and subscribing. Sometimes the behavior is a preliminary to purchase such as going to a car showroom or making a telephone inquiry. Advertising campaigns vary in *effectiveness*, i.e. how much change they achieve, and also in *efficiency*, i.e. how much effect they achieve for a given cost. A useful discussion of effectiveness and efficiency in advertising is provided by Ambler and Broadbent (2000).

In the commercial arena, three particular outcomes may be derived from advertising. These are that:

- Buyers pay more per unit and thus increase the profit on a sale.
- Buyers buy more than they would have done without the advertising. This occurs either because *more people buy* or because *existing buyers buy more*. It can also occur when advertising holds back a sales decline that would otherwise have happened.
- Costs are reduced.

Examples of these three outcomes are examined in more detail in later sections. The effect of ads on margins, sales and costs is often achieved by assisting other aspects of the marketing mix, for example, when ads amplify the effect of discounts. Ad effects can occur in a roundabout manner. In particular, advertising may:

- Induce word-of-mouth and media comment that eventually results in purchase.
- Increase retailer stocking, raising the opportunity to purchase. For example, the Felix cat food campaign (Broadbent 2000) boosted distribution so that a third of the extra sales effect came from this source. Similarly, advertising

for Terry's Chocolate Orange seemed to halt a decline in distribution (Broadbent 2000)[1]. In many cases, an enlarged distribution will produce a sales gain without the help of advertising.

- Set barriers to market entry by competitors, thereby reducing competition and retaining sales.
- Raise demand for scarce items such as property and shares. In the case of the One2One (now T-mobile) telephone company, ads lifted share values so that capital could be raised at lower cost, as (Kendall 1998).

This account of advertising effectiveness focuses directly on behavior because this is where revenue is derived and profits can be made. In the past, the assessment of advertising was related more to whether it was understood and recalled, and whether brand awareness and the intention to buy were increased. These conditions were claimed to mediate between the reception of the ad and any eventual purchase. To a degree, this mediation does occur but too much faith has been put in effects such as ad recall. States of mind may help to bring about behavioral changes but they make no profit on their own.

But sometimes consumer attitudes and beliefs do not correspond with the reality of the product offering, and campaigns may be needed to alter public opinion. In the early 1990s, the UK supermarket group, Tesco, was perceived as offering low prices and commensurately low quality, despite objective evidence that the quality was high. Public opinion reflected Tesco's past rather than its present performance. This poor perception of Tesco's quality probably held back growth and was, for this reason, the target of a sustained campaign designed to improve Tesco's standing in the eyes of customers (Broadbent 2000).

Also in the United Kingdom, the expansion of Skoda car sales was blocked by poor brand perception. The ad campaign directly confronted the low opinion of the Skoda brand among British car buyers and now Skoda cars have become much more popular (Rimini 2003). In Australia, Vodaphone is quite a small brand and initial advertising addressed the low awareness of Vodafone compared to Telstra and Optus (*Effective Advertising 5*, 2000). This may have helped the later growth of Vodaphone; when numbers in the category doubled, Vodaphone quadrupled its customers (*Effective Advertising 6*, 2001).

So, attitudes may be legitimate targets for advertising but what makes them legitimate is their link to profit-related behavior. The Tesco case would never have been discussed as a success if the new customers and extra sales had not materialized.

Price Support

Evidence

Some ads make consumers aware of discounts and the possibility of saving money. As might be expected, such price-related advertising tends to be associated with lower prices and leads to increased price sensitivity on the part of the consumer (Bolton 1989, Kaul and Wittink 1995). When this occurs, margins are squeezed and benefits must come via increased sales. By contrast, most brand advertising is designed to raise perceptions of quality and thus increase the appreciation of the brand. This sort of advertising tends to reduce price sensitivity, which allows the brand owner to raise margins. Studies reported in the *Advertising Works* series show many price-support effects, for example:

- Felix cat food and the Lurpak butter cases (Broadbent 2000). In the latter case, it was possible to show that price sensitivity dropped in the regions that received more advertising.
- A Colgate advertising campaign in the United Kingdom was associated with a 15 percent margin improvement when compared with the European average for toothpaste prices, and Olivio raised the average price, as well as sales, when it advertised (Kendall 1998).

Further evidence that advertising can support prices came from a study of the top five brands in 100 categories (Hamilton, East and Kalafatis, 1996). In this study, well-advertised brands usually had either a slightly lower price elasticity or were more highly priced than others[2]. The research showed that brand leaders advertised twice as heavily as follower brands and the main difference in price sensitivity occurred between leader and follower brands. This combination of high adspend and high price is a common pattern for leading brands (Farris and Reibstein 1991). Some part of this association may arise because successful high-margin brands have more cash to spend on advertising, i.e. the advertising is a consequence of the brand's success. However, the case histories that have been cited provide quite good evidence that advertising reduces price sensitivity. In the United Kingdom, the Andrex and Stella Artois cases further illustrate how brands can maintain margins with the help of advertising (see boxes).

The Andrex and Stella Artois cases show how good advertising can help a sound product to sell at a high price compared with other brands of similar quality. Another instance of this was the Renault Clio case (Duckworth 1997). In addition to selling well from 1991-5, the Clio maintained a price that was 13 percent above the average in its sector.

Andrex

The performance of Andrex toilet paper up to the start of 1992 has been evaluated by Baker (1993). This brand has led the field in the United Kingdom and is heavily advertised. When the competitive Kleenex Velvet toilet tissue was introduced in the early 1980s, consumers preferred it to Andrex on blind test but, despite this, Andrex held its market share. In 1992, when improvements had been made to the product, the two brands were equally rated on blind test but Andrex was much preferred when the name was visible, showing the strength of the brand.

Andrex, with a market share of 25%, has consistently outsold Kleenex, which had only 10% share. Despite recession and competition from 'green' brands, it has been priced above its rivals; this price premium was about 25% in 1990-91. This case indicates that advertising can be used to raise both margin and sales.

After 1993, Andrex suffered. The competition from high quality private label at lower prices was severe but Andrex still had about 20% market share at the end of the millennium, indicating the continuing strength of the brand.

Stella Artois

Price support from advertising has also been demonstrated by the success of Stella Artois in Britain (Baker 1993). Stella was advertised as 'reassuringly expensive', thus implying high quality. It attracted a large proportion of lager drinkers and secured a trade price premium of 7.5%. Publicans more than recovered this premium when they sold Stella at its higher retail price. Despite this evidence of popularity, Baker (1993) reported that, on blind test, Stella was not significantly preferred.

Broadbent (2000) took up the story. As recession took hold, 'reassuringly expensive' became a little too 'up-front' and Stella was repositioned as of 'supreme quality and therefore expensive'. In 1998-9, Stella was the leader in the premium lager market and, subsequently, it has made further gains on its two nearest competitors, Budweiser and Kronenbourg. In 1999, Stella Artois was the fifth largest grocery brand by value, having climbed from 23rd position in 1997. Also, Stella was priced 14% above the premium lager average.

The review in Broadbent (2000) explains that publicans who stock only one premium lager want the one that most of their drinkers prefer and this makes the market difficult for secondary brands. The case analysis suggests that the most recent advertising produced a profit increment that was six times the ad cost.

Mela, Gupta and Lehmann (1997) studied the impact of brand advertising and sales promotion on price sensitivity over an eight-year period. They focused on a mature product where life-cycle effects were minimal. They found that *reductions* in brand advertising were associated with *increased* price sensitivity, which implies that advertising increases price tolerance. Most of this effect occurred among the less brand loyal customers. Thus Mela *et al.* show that the price support from advertising occurs mainly because it affects buyers with low loyalty[3]. This research implies that loyal customers are of great value to a supplier because they are fairly impervious to the ads of competitors.

Squeezing the Retailer

So far we have not distinguished between the margins of the retailer and those of the manufacturer. Steiner (1973, 1993) reported on the effects of manufacturers' advertising in the toy industry and showed how brand advertising can reduce retailer margins whilst raising manufacturer margins. He found that the ads created a consumer demand for products, which compelled retailers to stock them; at the same time competition between retailers reduced their margin. Because of demand, manufacturers could increase *their* margin but the price to the consumer could fall because of the pressure on retailer margins. Farris and Albion (1980) reviewed this subject and concluded that advertising generally exerted pressure on retailers' margins and that the net effect of such advertising often lowered the price to the consumer[4]. When retailers have great power, as in the case of supermarkets in the United Kingdom, the 'Steiner' effect may be less apparent, but see the box on *power brands*.

When Supply is Limited

In free markets, increased demand for manufactured goods can be met by more production. When supply is relatively fixed, as in auctions and the sale of houses, increased demand will result in an increase in price. In equity markets, where the available stock is fixed in the medium term, corporate advertising may have a direct effect on the share price. Evidence for this effect is sketchy but Moraleda and Ferrer-Vidal (1991) showed that advertising raised the intention to apply for shares in the Spanish oil company, Repsol, in the run-up to privatization. It seems likely that advertising can stimulate demand for a public offering of shares, which allows the price of the shares to be set a little higher.

> **Power Brands**
> Steiner's work illustrates how manufacturers can sometimes overcome the control of the retailer by appealing directly to the consumer via advertising. If the manufacturer can ensure that consumers will not accept an alternative to their brand, the retailer must stock it. In the 1990s, this could have been one of the reasons for the focus on a reduced number of *power brands* by Procter and Gamble, and Unilever. However, the publicized reasons for deleting small brands centered on efficient production and distribution.

In monopoly situations, customers may feel exploited and see a product as poor value if they have to buy it. Here, advertising can be used to raise the perceived value. A study reported by Kendall (1998) showed how ads were used to address the low evaluation of North West Water in the United Kingdom (where water companies have monopolies). Before the advertising, customers were hostile to the company and objected to increases in their water costs. The advertising drew attention to the benefits offered by the company and raised the perceived value of the service. Customer satisfaction with the company also increased.

The Sales Response to Advertising

The cases in the *Advertising Works* and *Effective Advertising* series demonstrate that advertising can increase sales. On rare occasions the effect is large, as in the case of Levi 501 jeans in the United Kingdom. Here, campaigns from 1984 to 1987 raised sales 20 times (Feldwick, 1990). In other European countries, similar campaigns produced impressive sales gains for Levi (Baker, 1993). But the Levi 501 case was quite exceptional. Even when the best campaigns are reviewed, a gain of 100 percent or more is uncommon. In *Advertising Works 10* (Kendall 1998), only two out of the seventeen campaigns (for Olivio and Polaroid) showed a gain of over 100 percent over two years; in both cases, the gains were made easier by an initially small sales base and Rimini (2003) reports an annual increase in Olivio sales of less than 9 percent in later years. Really large gains in sales from advertising are also scarce in Australian reports; one of the best results in *Effective Advertising 5* showed that Listerine doubled sales over three and a half years and raised profit by 80 percent.

One very successful campaign in the UK was conducted by the ad agency, TBWA, for Wonderbra (see Figure 1.1). This was a low-budget campaign using billboard and magazine media (Baker 1995). The cost of the initial four-month campaign was £330,000 and this must rank as one of the most efficient ever assessed. Over a two-year period, gains in sales of 120 percent were achieved although Wonderbra was selling above the price of many other brands. The key to this success was almost certainly the substantial comment that the advertising provoked. It was calculated that the public relations value of this comment was worth over £17 million. Beside selling bras, it made an unknown model, Eva Herzigova, famous and Trevor Beattie, the creative director of the campaign, became a celebrity in the British ad industry.

The *Advertising Works* cases are selected because they are successful. Most advertising for established brands produces far less sales response. This is illustrated by a report by Riskey (1997) on 23 Frito-Lay ads. This study compared brand sales when ads were running with a no-ad control condition. The study was conducted using the BehaviorScan method of Information Resources Inc (IRI), which is described in more detail in Chapter 2. Twelve ads showed effects and these cases produced an average sales increase of 15 percent. The ads for the brands with small market shares were the most effective.

Figure 1.1. Wonderbra ad featuring Eva Hertzigova (by permission of TBWA)

Other work by IRI on upweights also indicates the moderate scale of ad effect. In the IRI studies, households receiving 50-100 percent extra advertising were compared with households receiving the normal weight (Lodish and Lubetkin 1992). Despite a possible selection bias (see next box), about half of the tests showed no sales effect. When there was an effect, the average increase in sales was 22 percent extra sales in the year of the upweight. However, advertising effects may last for a year or more (discussed in Chapter 3 under *Decay of Effect*) and such extended effects can add to the sales benefit from a campaign.

Weight Tests

Weight tests are conducted for two reasons: to see whether the copy is worn out and to find out whether heavier use of advertising will bring a greater return. In both cases, the brands must be fairly large since it is difficult to justify the cost of such testing for small brands. This means that those brands that are tested will not be representative of brands in general.

About half of weight tests show more sales as a result of more adspend and, of these, about two in five show enough gain to justify extra spending on advertising. But advertisers should be cautious about spending more on ads lest they prompt a competitor response that nullifies any sales gain.

Advertising often permits an increase in both sales and price. This double advantage occurred in the Stella Artois, Levi jeans and Wonderbra cases reviewed in this Chapter. When this occurs, the advertising has a substantial effect on profitability.

Large gains are quite often found in social applications of advertising. For example, a £1 million campaign to raise rear seat belt usage in the United Kingdom gave a directly quantifiable return of £18 million, and, when further assumptions were made about the costs of injury and death, the return was £73 million (Broadbent 2000). Another campaign in Australia achieved a drop in smoking of over 7 percent, equivalent to 190,000 fewer smokers. The healthcare saving was $24 million (*Effective Advertising 6*, 2001).

It is quite common to find no sales gain at all from advertising. The consumption of many categories is near-stationary and this means that any sales gain by one brand must usually be matched by losses among other brands. In such competitive markets, ads can be effective if they prevent sales losses. However, this explanation for no measurable effect can be too easy an excuse. Usually, competitive campaigns are not contemporaneous and, if the ad for the focal brand is effective, it should be possible to detect an increase in sales when it is broadcast, followed by a decline in sales as competitors reassert themselves. If this is not apparent it is unlikely that the ad is having any effect. Fulgoni (1987) has argued that many weight-test failures occur because the ads are ineffective.

> *Keys to Success?*
> The wide variation in the effectiveness of ads has led to speculation among
> practitioners about which elements of the ad make it effective. It might be thought
> that copy tests would isolate the key factors but, although these tests show that one
> copy is often superior to another, any useful recipes for success are hard to find.
> Mostly, the key elements that are suggested cite rather obvious features of an ad.
> For example, Moldovan (1984) focused on ad credibility and Brown (1986) on the
> power of the ad to arrest attention; later Brown (1991) stressed the degree to which
> the ad involved the potential purchaser with the brand. These claims are sensible
> but they are of limited value to those trying to create good copy. The creative
> aspect of advertising seems to be very important for sales success but, by its nature,
> this is not easily specified.

Reducing Costs

Successful advertising can reduce *unit* costs when increased volume is sold through the same distribution system. But, in some cases, the advertising can produce efficiencies that reduce *total* cost. For example, Volkswagen saved on storage costs when extra demand meant that they had fewer cars unsold (Kendall 1998). Costs may also be saved when advertising is accurately targeted and irrelevant inquiries are avoided. This was something Scoot.com learned when they first advertised; many calls produced no business and cost money (Broadbent 2000). This problem is particularly relevant to both industrial and personnel advertising where unproductive responses need to be avoided. Internet job advertising can get replies from anywhere in the world and should be designed to cut out applicants who cannot be appointed by virtue of their location or nationality. Also, when a product is physical rather than digital, it must be delivered, and the cost and complication of international delivery may make it desirable to use advertising that excludes some international customers.

Kendall (1998) showed the value of well-targeted advertising in the campaign to recruit personnel to the British Army. In 1994, one person from every 6.7 inquirers was enlisted. Following the advertising campaign, the conversion ratio improved to 1 in 3.4. In the analysis, it was estimated that this ratio change saved the Army £16 million after deducting the cost of the advertising. In addition, it appeared that better recruits were enlisted since they were less likely to drop out during the period of initial training.

Summary

*Advertising is **effective** to the extent that it changes target behavior in the desired direction; it is **efficient** when these gains are achieved at low cost.*

*Social advertising may target behaviors such as smoking, wearing seat belts and eating healthy foods. Commercial advertising targets behaviors that affect profit such as purchase, rental, and enrolment. The sales benefit from advertising may be realized as an increase in the **number** of sales or as an increase in **margin** when advertising encourages customers to tolerate a higher price. Often, advertising is used to support both a sales and a price increase. On rare occasions ad campaigns can more than double sales but mostly gains are modest if they occur at all. When there is no visible effect from advertising, it may prevent a sales loss or margin erosion that would otherwise have occurred. Advertising can also reduce the advertiser's **costs**.*

Notes

1. Rimini (2003), Broadbent (2000) and Kendall (1998) are the twelfth, eleventh and tenth volumes in the *Advertising Works* series, which is produced by the Institute of Practitioners in Advertising (IPA) in the UK; this series is published jointly with NTC, now part of the World Advertising Research Center (WARC). One volume is produced every two years. The cases describe how successful campaigns have been conducted and pay particular attention to the evidence for ad effectiveness and the return from advertising investment. The Advertising Federation of Australia organizes a similar review of good cases; their *Effective Advertising 5* was published in 2000 and *Effective Advertising 6* in 2001.

2. Price elasticity is the ratio of the proportionate increase in sales to the proportionate decrease in price. Because the decrease is negative, the elasticity is usually negative.

3. Loyalty is measured here as the share-of-category spending that a consumer gives to a brand; this is also known as *share-of-category requirement (SCR)*.

4. Economists have given attention to whether advertising is informational, and thus aids exchange, or whether it is a cost, thus adding to price. This debate ignores the different types of advertising (i.e. price and brand) and does not address the long-term impacts of advertising on the structure of markets. One possible structural effect of advertising is to produce more market concentration, i.e. fewer brands in a category, which can bring economies of scale.

Chapter 2
ADVERTISING FREQUENCY AND CONCENTRATION

*What is the sales response of consumers when they receive additional exposures to an ad? The evidence mostly shows **diminishing** sales increments with each extra exposure. However, some research has shown increased sales per exposure **if the ads are close together in time**. Explanations for this effect are discussed.*

Schedules

TV advertising can be scheduled in concentrated bursts that are separated by periods with little or no advertising, or it can be aired more continuously. Figure 2.1 shows how the same amount of advertising can be deployed in three alternative schedules.

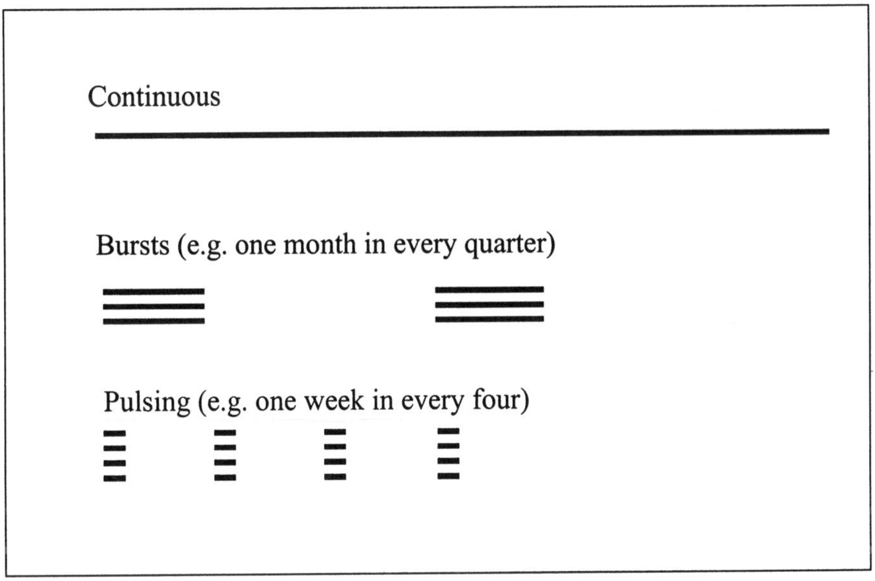

Figure 2.1. TV advertising schedules

The nature of the schedule affects the proportion of the audience that sees the ad (known as *reach, coverage,* or *penetration*) and also produces different *frequencies* of exposure in the households that do receive the ad. The effect of advertising depends on the penetration and frequency so, indirectly, schedules affect advertising response.

In order to use the best schedule, we need to know how individuals respond to additional ad exposures and how they react to the same number of exposures when these are concentrated in different time intervals. Work in this field has been hampered by the poor quality of the data and the techniques of analysis that were used. In the past, inferences were made from ad recall and other non-behavioral measures, which, as we will see, are poorly related to sales. Now, with actual sales data on individual respondents and better analysis, the effect of an extra exposure can be measured in terms of its effect on sales.

The Individual Response to Ad Exposures

If each additional exposure produces a smaller sales gain than the last; the response is *concave to the x-axis* and is an example of the economists' famous law of *diminishing marginal returns*. If this occurs, the most cost-effective number of exposures, (i.e. the *effective frequency*), is *one* and the best policy is to use a continuous schedule that spreads the advertising across the target population as widely and evenly as possible. In this way, more people are reached at lower frequencies. But if additional exposures produce at first increasing and then decreasing increments in sales, which is an *S-shaped* or *logistic* response curve, then the best strategy is to use a schedule that takes the audience quickly to the point where their sales response is steepest. This strategy sacrifices penetration for frequency. It may be achieved by schedules that use bursts followed by low-level advertising (drip) designed to keep the recipient at the optimum point on the response curve. Figure 2.2 shows the concave and S-shaped response curves.

S-Shaped or Concave Response?

Multiple showings of an ad produce different frequencies of exposure for different audience segments so that it is hard to infer from aggregate effects what the individual exposure pattern has been. For this reason, better understanding of ad effects comes from using single-source data, i.e. data on the exposures and purchases of single households (Broadbent, Spittler and Lynch 1997). Some early single-source work used studies of direct response to compare response to successive mailings (Pomerance and Zielske 1958, Zielske 1959). Simon (1979) reanalyzed data from Zielske's study and found that the second and later exposures gave diminishing returns. In further evidence, Simon and Arndt (1980) reviewed 37 advertising studies and found that the great majority showed a concave response function.

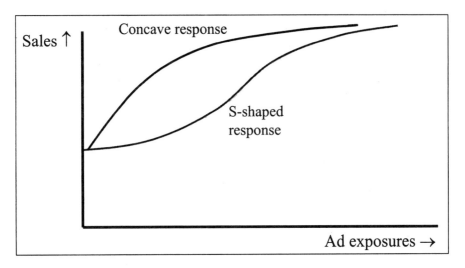

Figure 2.2. Concave and S-shaped responses to exposures

Although Simon and Arndt concluded that the incremental response to advertising generally became less with each exposure, they were at pains to point out the considerable methodological difficulties of research in this field. In particular, there is a problem posed by the decay of any ad effect as the period of time between exposure and measurement increases. Also, a given number of exposures can occur over different periods of time, thus varying the concentration. Broadbent (1998) pointed out that there is very little agreement among researchers and practitioners on the period over which exposures should occur when frequency effects are studied. For example, three exposures could occur in a day, a week, or the average inter-purchase interval, which is the mean lapse of time between purchases of the category by households[1].

Although much research evidence on exposures has pointed to a concave sales response function, these methodological problems leave room for doubt. Also, there are good reasons why the response to exposures may be S-shaped. One argument uses the idea of *breakthrough*, i.e. the need to concentrate ads so that they break through the clutter of other advertising and get over an attention threshold so that the audience cannot miss them (Broadbent 1998).

A second rationale for an S-shaped response pattern came from Krugman's (1972) 3-hit theory. Krugman argued that on first exposure viewers are curious, on the second the meaning of the ad may be clarified and they endorse or reject the message, and on the third and subsequent exposures they are reminded of the message again. In this account, the second and third exposures are more effective than the first. This thinking was crystallized in an influential book on effective frequency by Naples (1979), in which the 3-hit theory was presented as the basic rule.

Also supporting an S-shaped response function was a sophisticated analysis by Tellis (1988), which indicated an optimum weekly exposure frequency of two or three. Tellis (1997) argues that the effective frequency varies and depends upon three factors: brand familiarity, message complexity, and message novelty. Furthermore, a major analysis of IRI data (Lodish and Lubetkin 1992) indicated that both new and established products did better when the advertising was initially concentrated rather than spread over time. This evidence suggests that exposures need to exceed some threshold level if they are to have optimum effect.

McDonald (1995a) argued that the true pattern of sales response to advertising exposures is concave for mature brands and that his earlier work (McDonald 1970) supported this when re-analyzed. McDonald was influenced in part by work done by Jones on single-source data (1995a, 1995b, 1995c), which showed little gain after the first exposure. Even so, McDonald has remained cautious about frequencies, preferring two to one but seeing the optimum as contingent on the advertising context. McDonald argues that multiple exposures may be needed to exceed the exposure rates of competitive brands, i.e. to achieve breakthrough. This strategy implies that the appropriate frequency is contingent on the level of advertising by competitors in the category.

Although the doctrine that *'once is enough'* has become accepted among some research-oriented practitioners, a survey by Leckenby and Kim (1994) found that the great majority of US ad agencies used a '3-plus' rule and it is likely that this is still the favored practice. Rossiter and Percy (1997, ch16) review the management problems in this area.

There is more agreement between researchers and practitioners on ad frequency when the advertising or product is unusual. It is widely held that learning is built up with the first few exposures of an unusual ad so that a linear or S-shaped response may be expected under these conditions. Broadbent (1999) described an example of a novel ad campaign in which the sales response was initially low. In this case, the advertising introduced the character of Clive the leopard, who was used to represent the Schweppes brand. Those who were exposed to the advertising took some time to get used to Clive as the personification of the brand. Ad effect may also build up when the ads cause public discussion so that people look out for them and give them more attention, e.g. Benetton's use of shocking pictures of a dying AIDS sufferer or the advertising for Wonderbra illustrated earlier.

Jones' Work on STAS

The work of John Philip Jones (1995a, 1995b, 1995c) drew much attention when it was first presented. Jones compared households receiving one or more exposures, the *ad-exposed*, with those receiving none, the *ad-less*, and he counted the number of households buying the brand in the following seven days in these two groups. He calls the ratio of purchases between exposed and ad-less households *Short Term Advertising Strength* (STAS) and indexes this on 100. Thus a STAS score of 110 means that the exposed group buys 10 percent more than the ad-less group.

The key problem in this approach, explained by Broadbent (1995, 1998) and Lodish (1997, 1998), is that the Nielsen data used by Jones are a record of *naturally occurring* exposures (often termed '*as it falls*' data). Such data lack experimental control. In an experiment, equivalent groups are subjected to different levels of exposure and, because the groups are equivalent, any difference in the sales of the advertised brands can be attributed only to the exposure difference. When a difference in exposure occurs naturally between two households, it is likely to be associated with a difference in audience characteristics such as the level of television watching or employment status. In these circumstances, the concave response might simply reflect different audience composition at different exposure levels.

One audience characteristic that is associated with frequency is the proportion that buys the advertised brand. Buyers of a brand tend to be exposed to ads for the brand more often. This is called *purchase/viewing bias* and occurs partly because advertisers target ads towards buyers of the brand since these people respond better. Advertising for a brand is often associated with concurrent sales promotions and competitor advertising; Jones' method does not separate out the effect on sales of such co-varying factors. In consequence, these problems mean that inferences made using Jones' method are unreliable (see the box on the STAS controversy).

Jones' work created a demand for better methods of exposure research and these have begun to emerge. For example, Roberts (1996) conducted a study that controlled for co-varying promotion and purchase/viewing bias. He found that the response curve was concave in 15 out of 17 cases using established brands. In five out of seven cases where the brand was new or re-launched the response was effectively linear.

The STAS Controversy

Jones' work raised much comment and criticism. Among others, Broadbent (1995) expressed doubts but Jones (1995d) stuck to his position and reiterated this in a further paper (Jones and Blair 1996).

The STAS method was evaluated using data from the IRI BehaviorScan research (see next box). Schroeder, Richardson and Sankaralingam (1997) set out to test whether seven brands showed sales volume gains from advertising that corresponded with Jones' STAS scores. Schroeder *et al.'s* work is summarized by Lodish (1997). STAS is a measure based on purchase occasions whereas the BehaviorScan analysis is based on sales volume, adjusted for covariates, and is experimental. STAS values were calculated from the IRI data and these were of similar range to those found by Jones. These values were compared with BehaviorScan measures of ad effect that included corrections for bias. There was a modest relationship between the STAS and BehaviorScan results. The R^2 value was 24% and, in a comparison such as this, a better fit is needed to vindicate STAS. Lodish showed that the modest relationship was related to biases in the STAS measure and concluded that "STAS measures may be too simplistic and imprecise to generate 'new empirical knowledge'".

Jones (1998) accepted neither the evidence from Schroeder *et al.* (1997) nor the criticisms of Lodish (1997). He claimed that his design, comparing exposed and ad-less households, was experimental. Lodish (1998) responded and stated again why Jones' design failed to meet experimental criteria.

Concentration

Roberts (1999) has provided fresh evidence on the role of concentration. He used a UK dataset on 750 households in Taylor Nelson Sofres' Superpanel gathered by TVSpan. Each household was equipped with a TV 'setmeter' so that viewing could be recorded. Ad exposures were related to household purchases recorded through Superpanel. One hundred and thirteen brands from ten categories were studied. These were advertised over a two-year period from March 1996 to March 1998. This method produces 'as it falls' data so care must be taken to reduce the effects of biases. Roberts controlled for concurrent sales promotions; also he divided households by weight of television viewing and analyzed these segments separately before recombining the results. In this way, biases associated with heavy and light viewing were reduced. Roberts also compared respondents who had received exposures with *these same respondents* when, at another time, they had not received any ad exposures for 28 days. This comparison addresses (but does not fully resolve) a major problem associated with Jones' STAS procedure, that the exposed and ad-less households have different characteristics. Thus,

Roberts' work should give a better indication of any ad effect.

BehaviorScan

The inhabitants of Au Claire, Wisconsin, have cable television because off-air reception is poor. Information Resources Inc (IRI) uses Au Claire and four other similarly cabled towns to test ads. Households are recruited to a panel and agree to receive television that may be modified by IRI. The BehaviorScan technology swaps commercials so that some households receive a trial ad or extra exposures of a normal ad when compared with other households. The former allows copy tests to be conducted, the latter weight tests. Members of the panel show an identification number when they buy groceries in town. IRI finances the scanners in the town's stores and downloads sales information each night from these scanners. This system allows sales to be tied to households receiving different frequencies of advertising. Malec (1982) describes the system in more detail. GfK has used the same technology in Germany (Litzenroth 1991).

IRI found that their consumer panels were representative of spending in the local community and that the communities were close to national patterns of expenditure for the brands tested.

This powerful system permits experimental tests but suffers from some weaknesses:
- Members of the household may not be watching a TV set when it is on.
- Out-of-town purchases (out-shopping) are missed.
- The tests exclude trade response. National advertising may generate more retailer stocking and competitor advertising than in the test communities.
- The brands that are tested are chosen for commercial reasons and this may bias the sampling.
- There may be a 'hothouse' effect if panelists guess that commercials are on test and, as a consequence, take more interest in them.

Roberts (1999) conducted a number of analyses. Here, we focus on the effects of 1, 2 or 3 exposures in three different intervals: one day, three days and twenty-eight days. Figure 2.3 shows the sales recorded *after the end of the exposure interval*. When the exposures occur over 28 days the additional effect of the second and third exposure is small and follows the familiar concave pattern. When all three exposures occur in the same day (and in practice this is often a few hours) the effect of the second and third exposures is large and produces an accelerating sales response which could be the lower part of an S-curve. Over 3 days, the pattern is approximately linear. This seems like a real advance on our knowledge of how multiple exposures work. There appears to be an interaction between exposures when these are close together in time. We may speculate that the first exposure alerts or *primes* the respondent so that later exposures are noticed and processed more (but see the box on explaining the effect of concentration). When the interval is longer, any alerting may subside before the next exposure.

The sales effects in Figure 2.3 need some interpretation. Purchase is measured immediately after the exposure time interval has elapsed. If the exposure interval is short (1-day or 3-day) there is less time for any ad effect to decay before sales are measured. Over 28 days, there will be substantial decay of the first and second exposures before measurement of sales impact. This helps to explain the large difference in purchase effect shown between 3 exposures in a day and 3 exposures in 28 days. Figure 2.4 shows that the long-term sales effect of three or more ads in one day is somewhat larger than the effect of three ads or more received over a longer period.

In an unpublished analysis, Roberts assesses how concentration might affect sales under the three schedules illustrated in Figure 2.1. When the potential sales effect is calculated, one-month bursts perform worst and one-week pulsing is best. The degree of superiority of pulsing over the continuous schedule is estimated to be from 4 to 13 percent depending on the total weight of advertising employed. This analysis does not make any assumptions about the schedules of competitors. Presumably, any gains would be negated if competitors adopted the same schedule.

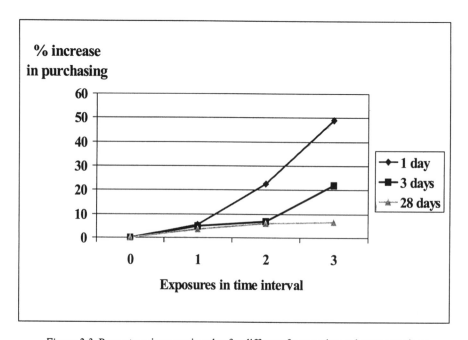

Figure 2.3. Percentage increase in sales for different frequencies and concentrations

Explaining the Effect of Concentration

How do we explain the stronger effect of ad exposures when they are concentrated into a short period? Two processes could be at work: *priming* and *breakthrough*.

Priming. If a series of positive adjectives is presented before the display of a photograph of a person, the evaluative judgments about the person are likely to be more positive. The adjectives prime a positive response. Priming is the activation of some cognitive or affective response so that it becomes temporarily more *accessible*. As a result it is more likely to be used in judgments and may steer behavior. Applying this thinking to ad concentration, initial exposures may prime thinking about the brand so that later ad exposures are more readily recognized and response strength is built up. Such a process is likely to occur when exposures are close together in time and the priming activation is not dissipated before the next exposure. Eagly and Chaiken (1993) provide a more detailed analysis of priming.

Breakthrough. This relates to the idea of *interference*, which occurs when a change in the strength of one idea affects the strength of another idea. In the competition between brands, more recent ads for Brand A tend to displace the propensity to buy Brand B by *retroactive interference*, i.e. the new learning about Brand A displaces the previously learned responses to buy Brand B. Prior ads for Brand B prevent this by *proactive interference*, i.e. previous learning makes it harder to acquire new learning that is similar to the previous learning. More concentrated exposure of ads for a brand should help it to displace another brand by retroactive interference since competitors are unlikely to present their advertising at comparable frequency and therefore, for a short period, the focal brand gets more *share-of-voice*. Also, background levels of all forms of advertising (called *clutter*) inhibit response to any ad and concentrated exposures may overcome this clutter, thus increasing *share-of-mind* for the focal brand. These interference effects are more apparent when the material that is remembered is trivial, which fits low-involvement advertising.

A study by Burke and Srull (1988) showed proactive and retroactive interference effects in the *recall* of advertising. In their study, the target brand ad frequency was manipulated from 1 to 3 exposures while competitive advertising was manipulated from 0 to 3 exposures. The study showed that, as competitive brand advertising was increased, the recall of target brand details decreased. The study showed that recall accelerated with exposures of the target brand when there was no competition but became concave when competition was high. These findings correspond with the concentration effect, observed by Roberts (1999), and suggest that Roberts' results could have been found because there is little or no interference from ads for competitive brands over short periods. A weakness of this study is that it was based on recall and lacked any observation of sales effect.

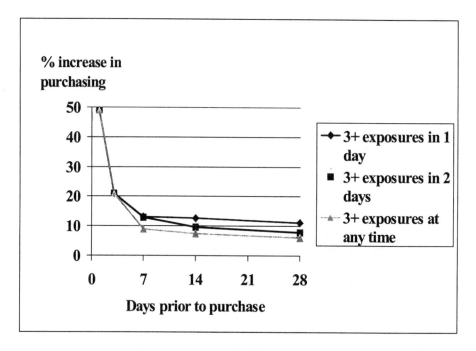

Figure 2.4. Some lasting effect of concentration

Roberts' evidence, though persuasive, is the first of its kind to be published and should be closely scrutinized. First, we note that the data are gathered in Britain where ad clutter is relatively low. This raises the possibility that stronger effects from concentration might be observed in high-clutter environments. Second, the study is restricted to groceries. Third, doubts may be felt about the effectiveness of the control comparison used in this work (the purchases made by the same respondents when they have not been exposed to the advertising for 28 days). However, in this study control subjects had to be 'in the market', i.e. they had to make purchases in other categories and this limits the discrepancies possible between control and test groups.

Summary

*The effect of advertising on a potential brand buyer depends on the number of exposures received in a period (**frequency**) and whether these exposures are **concentrated** or spread out over the period. The total effect of an ad campaign depends on these individual effects and on the proportion of the population exposed (**penetration, reach**). Frequency, concentration and* *penetration are affected when a given weight of advertising is delivered under different schedules. Because of this, the schedule can affect the campaign outcome.*

*To select the best schedule we need to understand how individuals react to different frequencies and concentrations. A key issue here is whether additional exposures produce diminishing effects or not. Although there is much evidence supporting diminishing effects there is also evidence against this, particularly when the advertising or the product is new or when social comment causes some 'snowballing' of interest. The evidence also indicates that, when television ad exposures are concentrated into a day or less, they produce a response pattern that initially increases with each exposure. Two reasons were offered for this concentration effect. One is that the earlier exposures **prime** the response to later exposures, making people more receptive. A second reason is that high exposure concentrations are less affected by **interference** from other advertising. If further evidence supports the concentration effect, advertising on TV may work better if advertisers adopt pulsing schedules (short concentrated periods followed by longer rest periods).*

Research in this field has been complicated by the poor quality of the data used and method of analysis. In particular, it is difficult to draw conclusions from non-experimental data without careful removal of associated biases. For this reason, the findings from STAS analyses have been questioned.

Notes

1. Purchase frequencies obviously differ by category but many grocery categories are bought in the region of eight to twelve times a year on average; this means that mean inter-purchase intervals of four to six weeks are common for many categories.

Chapter 3
WEAROUT, CARRYOVER EFFECTS AND DECAY OF ADVERTISING

*Ads **wear out** (i.e. cease to influence receivers) after a number of exposures and must then be replaced. To explain wearout we need a model that describes response to repeated exposures. The model presented in this Chapter specifies **primary** responses to advertising that may be either thoughtful or automatic, and **carryover effects** that induce further sales if there has been a sales effect at the primary stage. Carryover effects are persisting changes that occur in a number of ways: change in thinking (framing), purchase reinforcement (purchase is easier if it has been done before), impacts on the distribution system, and the influence of purchasers on other potential buyers.*

*When ads do have an effect, this effect **decays** over time. Research on the decay pattern now suggests that there are two components in this process, short-term and long-term.*

***Consumer segments** respond differently to TV advertising. Light viewers respond more than heavy viewers. Evidence is also reported on the response to ads of consumer segments with different weights of purchase and different loyalties to the advertised brand.*

Wearout

Wearout depends on a number of conditions. Here, we focus on the observed loss of effectiveness of advertising with repeated exposure. There is limited research in this field and, until recently, few dissented from Krugman's (1972) position. This was that ads would temporarily lose their effectiveness after a number of exposures but that, after a rest, the ads could be aired again and much of their effectiveness would then be restored. Only after several cycles of this sort would it be necessary to replace the ads. Figure 3.1 shows how this could work if there is no loss of sales between bursts.

A rather different emphasis comes from Jones and Blair (1996), and Blair and Rabuck (1998). They treat wearout as a consequence of the frequency effect and see little scope for recovery when the ad is rested. This would make the life of an ad relatively short. Sales gains from successive airings of the ad would come mainly from those who had not seen the ad before and this penetration growth would fall off quite quickly. To support their account, Jones and Blair present the sales evidence shown in Figure 3.2. This suggests that each successive burst has markedly less effect and, after three bursts, the brand is losing sales to the competition. However, to interpret Figure 3.2 we need to know how sales fall off between bursts; if any gains mostly decay between bursts, it could be argued that the advertising is continuing to work. The 'no recovery' argument is supported by Walling and Owen (2000), who again find that wearout is a simple function of exposure and that advertising did not recover when it was rested for a month.

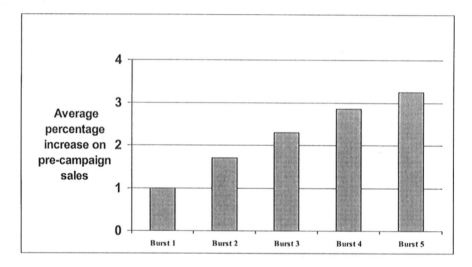

Figure 3.1. The Krugman hypothesis that ads recover if they are rested between bursts

Blair and Rabuck (1998) draw attention to an issue of commercial importance on which the evidence is mixed. A study of advertising designed to stimulate the milk consumption of children by the National Dairy Council (Baker 1995) indicated that copy should be replaced after 2000 TVRs, i.e. an average of 20 exposures for each TV household. Franzen (1994) suggested that 60 percent of effectiveness had gone after 1250 TVRs. Scott and Solomon (1998) report 13 studies with claims of wearout occurring after 2 to 18 exposures (average about 8). Naik (1999) assessed wearout as the duration of time required for the impact of the advertising copy to decline by half; this was three months in the case of a Levi Strauss product. These claims do not show much agreement. Also, any regular television viewer or radio listener can note that some ads are heavily repeated, producing exposures well in excess of those reported above. If wearout occurs after about eight exposures, much of this advertising expenditure is wasted. Can practitioners be that wrong?

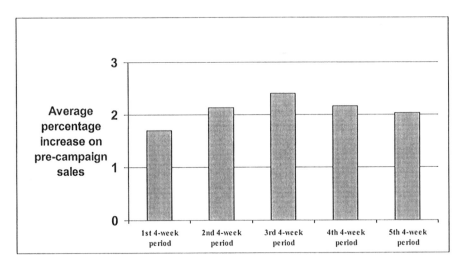

Figure 3.2. Evidence of wearout (from Blair and Rabuck 1998)

What Wears Out?

Most of us have favorite ads that we are willing to see time and time again. What is not clear in the case of these creative ads is whether they have a continuing sales effect. A review by Pechmann and Stewart (1988) looked at aspects of the ad that might affect wearout. They claimed that ads wear out faster if they relate to high involvement topics and that emotional appeals wear out more slowly than ads based on verbal arguments. Rossiter and Percy (1997) argue that 'transformational' ads last longer (i.e. ads for products with intrinsic rather than instrumental value). It is also widely accepted that print ads wear out faster than those on television.

Ad campaigns are built on themes. Jones and Blair (1996) claim that it is specific ads that wear out, not the whole campaign and its theme. They argue that new copy should not overthrow the basic strategy if it is working. Normally, new copy restates the basic proposition about a brand in a fresh way. Examples might be the way different Coca-Cola ads all express togetherness and mutual support or Audi ads focus on the quality of the car's engineering. These themes can be revisited in many ways.

Wearout helps to explain why increases in ad weight often have little or no effect. The extra weight may take exposures to the point where they no longer have much impact. Wearout effects show the importance of changing copy, a position endorsed by Lodish and Lubetkin (1992). Evidence in favor of variety in ad copy comes from studies by Adams (1916), and by Burnkrant and Unnava (1987). In both cases, the researchers compared three showings of different ads for a brand with three showings of the same ad. There was more effect on purchase propensity when the ads were different. It is interesting to note that one successful campaign for RACV motor insurance in Australia rotated five different ads over the week (*Effective Advertising 6,* 2001). Here, some of the campaign success may have stemmed from copy variety. But changing copy is expensive, particularly for television ads. One way of refreshing the copy is to create a serial with the same characters; this technique has been used in Britain and the United States to promote instant coffee. Another technique that could be cheaper would be to use the different 'takes' of the same ad since the small variations in execution might attract interest.

Multi-Media Plans

Other things being equal, copy will wear out more slowly if exposures are spread more widely across media since this reduces the average frequency of exposure. Also, there may be some synergy between media if an ad in one medium primes attention to corresponding ads in another medium. For example, a TV ad might create some interest in a car model, which could then be satisfied by the detail in a print ad or on a website. Some benefit from multi-media plans was claimed in a series of nine studies in different countries (Confer 1992). In this research, better results were obtained when 30 percent of the budget was spent on print and 70 percent on television, compared with 100 percent on television. Another study indicated that there was a 15 percent gain in effectiveness when 10 percent of TV expenditure was diverted to radio (Ingram and Cory 2001). However, it is not clear that the variety of media is the basis for the improvement. It could be caused by more variety of copy and lower frequency, both leading to less wearout.

A Model of Advertising Effect

We need an account of advertising effect that explains the strong effect of early exposures as well as the continuing effect from what is often a large number of subsequent exposures (if common television scheduling practice is to be justified). Figure 3.3 illustrates a model in which advertising has two types of *primary* effect on an audience. In the model, the first presentation of an ad (or the first few presentations when there is a concentration effect) often secures more attention and may produce quite elaborate thinking by those who are exposed to it. It is likely that this more thoughtful initial response has a substantial sales effect when it occurs but that this is not usually repeated on later exposures when only the second primary effect occurs. This second primary effect takes the form of passive, low-involvement automatic mechanisms that help to maintain brand awareness (easily recognized and recalled) and favorably regarded. Mechanisms of this sort produce weak effects but may continue to work over many repetitions. This dual-process account of the primary effect of an ad is not original. Dual-process accounts appear in work on persuasion by Fazio (1990) and Petty and Cacioppo (1985), (see Chapter 4).

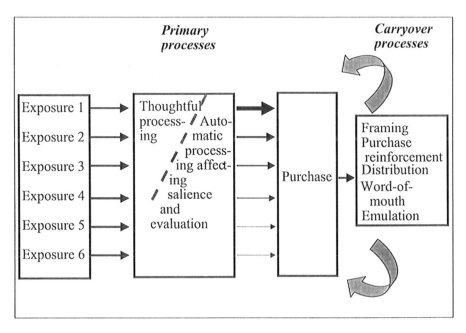

Figure 3.3. Primary and carryover responses to advertising

Carryover Sales Effects of Advertising

Figure 3.3 also shows carryover processes that arise as a result of the primary effects. These carryover effects on sales are generally weak but, because they are sustained over long periods of time, may contribute substantially to the total sales benefit from advertising. Studies of the connection between primary and carryover effects consistently show that carryover effects occur only when there is a sales effect at the primary stage. Abraham and Lodish (1990) reported that, if advertising tests do not show an effect after six months, they are unlikely to show any effect later. Jones (1995a) found that there were no one-year ad effects unless short-term effects were detected in the first seven days after exposure. Riskey (1997) observed that longer-term effects in 12 ad campaigns occurred only when there were shorter-term effects. Lodish *et al.* (1995b) found no delayed effects from ads that were ineffective in their test year. *This evidence shows that carryover effect is an outcome of primary effect, but a primary effect does not guarantee a carryover effect.*

The carryover effect could arise in a number of ways. One mechanism, called *framing*, is a persisting change in the way a product or brand is viewed. Some framing changes affect the way the product is categorized. For example, ice cream may be seen as an end-of-meal desert, as a self-indulgent snack or as high-cholesterol junk food. Health advertising that successfully implants the last view may produce long-term reductions in the amount of ice cream bought. Similarly, advertisers may persuade customers to think of plain black chocolate as an ingredient in cooking as well as a confectionery treat. Usually, the changes produced by advertising involve a more modest change in thinking that adjusts the positioning of the brand rather than its category; for example, ads may establish that a car model is more economical than previously thought. These shifts in thinking, whether dealing with the category or the attribute, are likely to be produced by the thoughtful primary processes rather than by automatic mechanisms.

Another process that could produce a carryover effect is *purchase reinforcement*. When a short-term ad effect induces extra purchase, this additional purchase experience may strengthen the propensity to buy the brand in the future. Effectively, loyalty is increased. Purchase reinforcement could be the consequence of an increase in brand accessibility (Fazio and Zanna 1981, Fazio, Powell and Herr 1983, Fazio 1986). Here, purchase makes it easier to think of the brand so that repeat purchase is facilitated. Purchase reinforcement could also be based on better knowledge of where to buy the brand (which store and where in the store). In their studies, Deighton (1984) and Givon and Horsky (1990) found that longer-term ad effects could be attributed to purchase reinforcement rather than to framing. But framing and purchase reinforcement may be mutually supportive. One possible arrangement, which combines framing and purchase reinforcement, is that advertising operates *after* consumption to change the understanding of the brand and/or the consumption experience; this effect of advertising has been shown by Braun (1999).

A third carryover effect occurs when advertising raises *distribution* and reduces *stockouts* so that the product is more easily purchased. Better stocking may occur either because retailers anticipate demand when they are advised about ad campaigns, or because the extra demand from an ad campaign forces retailers to increase stock. If improved distribution helps to raise sales, retailers may maintain the higher stock level after the advertising has finished.

A fourth process is social influence, either as positive *word of mouth* when consumers recommend the product to others or as *emulation* (copying) when publicly used products catch the fancy of others, as with fashion goods. Emulation requires no effort on the part of the primary user who is copied. Some services on the Internet have induced emulation; for example, the rapid and wide acceptance of Hotmail (any email on Hotmail carries a message at the end, promoting the service). Marketers use the term *viral* marketing to describe such processes.

The idea that new usage is often started by recommendation is undeniable. Services, in particular, are often introduced in this way. Despite this, word of mouth gets rather limited attention in advertising textbooks. What we want is an understanding of the customer factors connected with word of mouth that may be stimulated by advertising. This is addressed in detail later. For the present, we can see that ads may instigate recommendation by simulating social influence or by providing facts that can be used when people recommend. For example, a British ad for Lavazza coffee stated that it was the most popular coffee in Italy. This is a fact that is persuasive among people who respect Italians for their discrimination in food and drink and it is easily repeated. This suggests an important function for media that are good at imparting information (print, websites). If people discover facts for themselves in such media, they may feel they 'own' the knowledge and may be more willing to pass it on.

We have seen that carryover effects occur as the outcome of *sales* induced at the primary stage. However, what would happen if the supplier chose to take the advantage derived from advertising as an increase in *margin* instead of sales? Would the advantage that is seen in the short term continue as a carryover effect? The question is hypothetical but important. It seems likely that *framing* would produce a continuing effect; in framing, the ads alter the appeal of the brand and this effect should persist. Some increase in distribution-led sales may occur if retailers also benefit from a higher price. There could also be some effect from recommendation; if people like a brand more, they may be more willing to recommend it, but a high price could also inhibit recommendation. Other carryover effects could be lost if no extra sales occur as a primary response since there can be no extra purchase reinforcement or emulation. We need more evidence on this matter, but it appears that marketers could lose long-term sales if they take the benefit from advertising as a price increase.

Problems with Purchase Reinforcement

Two objections may be made to the purchase reinforcement explanation for the carryover effect of advertising. One is that there can be no such effect in the case of consumer durables; people who have just bought a new cooker are not in the market for another one. Because of this, Givon and Horsky (1990) suggest that advertising induces a different reinforcement effect for durables. They suggest that those who have received the advertising, and become potential adopters as a result, then derive knowledge about the product from those who have already adopted it. If this happens, it suggests that much effective advice is solicited by the recipient.

The second objection asks why an ad-induced increase in purchasing produces purchase reinforcement when extra sales from sales promotions generally show no appreciable carry-over effect, as found by Ehrenberg, Hammond and Goodhardt 1994). If anything, promotions *reduce* long-term repeat purchase (Guadagni and Little 1983, Lattin and Bucklin 1989). What is the difference between the purchase produced by ads and that produced by sales promotion? This brings us back to framing. The argument here is that good advertising produces a long-term change in the way that the product is regarded. In this way an ad could raise both current and later purchase levels but a discount only has an effect while it is in force since it does not produce any long-term change in thinking.

Word of Mouth

The academic study of word-of-mouth influence began with the 19th Century work of Gabriel Tarde (published in English in 1903). Tarde noted that the adoption of an innovation tended to follow an S-curve over time, as shown in Figure 3.4. Subsequently, Bass (1969) showed how the S-curve could be derived mathematically if the population was divided into innovators who had already adopted a new product (and who could therefore recommend it) and imitators, who were potential adopters. Since there are few adopters at first, take up is initially slow and an external influence such as advertising is required to start the process. The upswing in the first stage of the S-curve occurs as total recommendation rises with the increase in the number of users, while the eventual flattening of the S-curve occurs when there are few potential adopters left.

The modeling of new product adoption has been a mixed success and has disappointed those who want to use it to *predict* purchase diffusion (Mahajan, Muller and Bass 1990). One problem has been that the total adopting population is only known with confidence after the product has been widely accepted so that an essential input to the model is not available at an early stage when it is needed for predictive purposes.

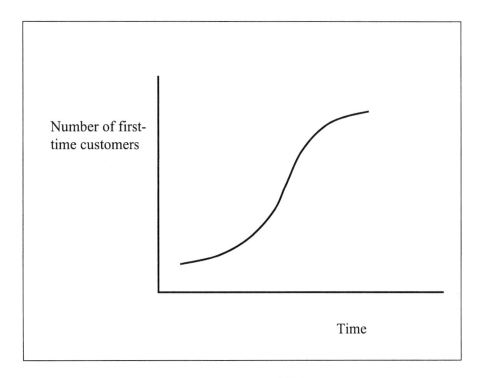

Figure 3.4. The S-shaped diffusion curve

In diffusion modeling, assumptions are made about the impact of recommendation at different stages of adoption. This impact depends on three conditions: the number of adopters who can recommend, the proportion of such persons who do recommend, and the effectiveness of their recommendation. All these conditions can change at each stage of the product's life cycle and diffusion models normally only incorporate the first condition. Such models would benefit from direct evidence on the rates of recommendation of adopters and the effectiveness of such recommendation.

An rather different approach to the study of social influence began with work by Lazarsfeld (1944). He showed that there was a two-step flow in mass communication with opinion leaders passing on information received from the mass media. Later work indicated that transmission could be multi-stage rather than two-stage and showed how social structure, group membership and opinion leadership facilitated the process (Rogers 1983). More elaborately, Gatignon and Robertson (1985, 1991), presented diffusion as a social process involving word of mouth, sub-group differences, product characteristics, marketing variables, and the adoption environment. However, this still gives limited attention to the specific effects of word-of-mouth communications and their centrality in diffusion suggests that we need a better understanding of the factors that predict word of mouth and the way word of mouth contributes to decisions.

Table 3.1. Main Channel Used to Choose a New Service (Kingston University, unpublished)

Product	Recomm-endation %	Personal Search %	Advertising/ Media %	Other %
Search engine	68	9	22	2
Email	60	26	14	0
Dentist	59	3	9	30
Leisure centre (subscription)	57	20	15	9
Favourite restaurant	55	38	3	4
ISP (consumer)	55	5	40	0
Education institution	49	19	2	30
Leisure centre (discount entry)	46	31	13	11
Optician	39	9	15	38
Auto servicing	36	6	4	52
Mobile phone service provider (students)	35	6	26	32
House contents insurance	33	2	44	21
Auto insurance	27	7	47	19
Mobile phone service provider	26	19	12	44
Main fashion store	23	54	4	16
ISP (industrial)	22	18	19	41
Auto insurance (recent switchers)	22	16	35	27
Dry cleaning	14	26	4	56
Auto purchase	13	42	13	33
Supermarket	9	22	8	62
Mean	**37**	**19**	**17**	**26**

The three main sources of influence on voluntary consumer behavior are word-of-mouth influence, personal search by the consumer, and the mass media. Table 3.1 shows the percentage of respondents citing these different channels as the principal influence in decisions about services and car purchase. These data come from unpublished studies conducted at Kingston University using convenience samples. The 'other' category reflects the fact that some service use is contractually obliged, and some choice depends on location or on accidental discovery.

Table 3.1 corresponds quite well with evidence gathered in the United States by Keaveney (1995), who found that recommendation was the main method for selecting a new service supplier in about 50 percent of cases while personal search and advertising communications were each cited by 20 percent of the sample.

In other research on the adoption of innovations, the dominant influence has been found to be word of mouth (Brown and Reingen 1987). In markets for well-established goods, word of mouth may have less effect but, even here, many products undergo development and the new features can be seen as innovations. For example, in recent years air conditioning in cars has been widely adopted in more temperate climates and social influence is likely to have played a part in this change.

The adoption of an innovation or the switching of brands involves some risk and word of mouth may reduce this risk. Lau and Ng (2000) argued that word of mouth is more important when the risk is high and Rosen and Olshavsky (1987) found that respondents were more reliant on the views of others if the product was high-risk or required more decision time. It is claimed that services are particularly risky since they cannot be tested like physical products. For this reason, would-be purchasers of services may seek reassurance from others before buying. An existing customer can take account of another person's needs when giving advice, and is thus well placed to reduce that person's uncertainty.

To some extent, this discussion of risk in services misses the point. There is quite a lot of risk in the purchase of physical products too; for example, electrical goods are rarely tried out before purchase so that uncertainty applies here. But when the product is a good, it is usually purchased from outlets that stock competitive brands so that the customer can compare alternatives as well as taking advice from sales staff. By contrast, service suppliers such as banks and dentists offer no alternatives so that the choice has to be made before close contact with the service delivery staff. Thus, it is difficult to assess many services in any way other than by word of mouth from existing customers. Word of mouth may also be important in goods choices where the goods are sold via single-brand outlets (e.g. Dell computers).

When we ask respondents how they chose a new product they may refer to the channel of information or to their specific need. Table 3.2 shows the main reason given when people were asked how they came to choose their current car. These reasons have been divided between those respondents who retained the same brand as before and those who switched to another brand. In Table 3.2, recommendation is not mentioned as a reason for retention but it gets a small role in choice when the buyer switches.

Table 3.2 suggests that there is one set of criteria that is used for deciding whether to stay with a brand. If that decision is negative, a new set of criteria is used for the choice of the new brand. The two sets have little in common. This indicates that switching decisions occur in stages, first there is a decision to abandon the old brand or not, then, if the old brand is dropped, there is a further decision on alternative brands. This is illustrated in Figure 3.5. If switching generally occurs according to these stages, we should separate *switching from* and *switching to*. Advertising designed to prevent switching from (customer retention) should have a different content from advertising designed to increase switching to (customer acquisition) because the needs of consumers in each case are different. From our limited data, recommendation seems relevant only to customer acquisition.

Table 3.2. Reasons for Retaining or Switching Car Brand (Francolini 1999)

Reasons for repurchase of same brand	N=138 %	Reasons for switching to new brand	N=162 %
Reliability	43	More money to spend	17
No choice	15	Needed bigger car	15
Safety	13	No choice	12
Economy	11	Good deal on old car	11
Performance	7	Old car unreliable	7
Holds value	5	Recommendation	7
Good size	2	Bad servicing	6
Comfortable	2	Other reasons	19

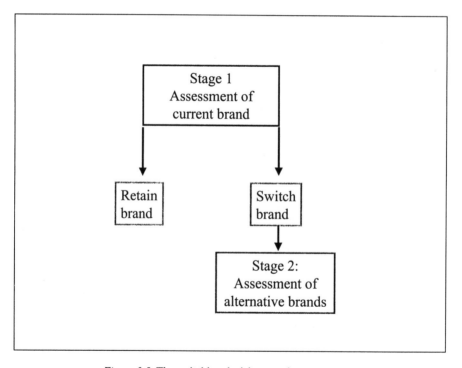

Figure 3.5. The switching decision may have two stages

Using Word of Mouth

If we want to use advertising to induce recommendation, we need to know how recommendation occurs. To some extent, research on the occurrence of word of mouth has been hampered by the assumption that it is the outcome of satisfaction. Recent work has helped to clarify this matter. Mangold, Miller and Brockway (1999) examined the circumstances under which word of mouth is produced. Respondents were asked to recall their positive and negative communications about services over the preceding six months and to relate how the word of mouth came about. The predominant circumstance (50 percent) was the *'felt need'* of the recipient, usually prompted by a request for information. The next most common circumstance (19 percent) was *'coincidental communication'* when the advice arose out of a conversation. The investigation showed that the communicator's *satisfaction or dissatisfaction* was a key reason in only 9 percent of the cases and the recipient's satisfaction or dissatisfaction was key in only 3 percent of the cases. This indicates that, although satisfaction may be an underlying condition in many instances of word of mouth, it is not sufficient on its own and other factors may be more important in prompting advice. Such factors include the circumstances of the person receiving any recommendation. For example, a user may recommend an Internet-based credit card to one person but not to another person who is less computer-literate. Or, advice may take account of the recipient's ability to afford the product.

So far we have established that recommendation is an important factor in consumer choice when the product is novel or is a service, and that satisfaction is only part of the explanation. Other possible causes of recommendation have been investigated and these have led to the model shown in Figure 3.6 (East and Lomax 2002). Though not fully tested, this model suggests that, like other behavior, recommendation depends on opportunity, motivation, and expertise. In addition, the model indicates that recommendation rates rise when the service is more prevalent in the environment or is made salient by the customer's frequent use.

In Figure 3.6, opportunities are partly explained by the number of social contacts. Some people, as Gladwell (2000) points out, have exceptionally wide networks of contacts. These people are difficult to locate but they are more common in certain occupations (taxi drivers, hairdressers), which may be used to target advertising. Figure 3.6 also suggests that marketing communications can assist recommendation by raising the attitude to the service (which means raising satisfaction), increasing expertise and by helping to keep the service salient. Here, the role of expertise is of interest because this is not normally emphasized in advertising. Ad copy that improves a person's knowledge about complex products may increase the chance that he or she will recommend those products. As noted earlier, this is a function well served by the print medium and by websites.

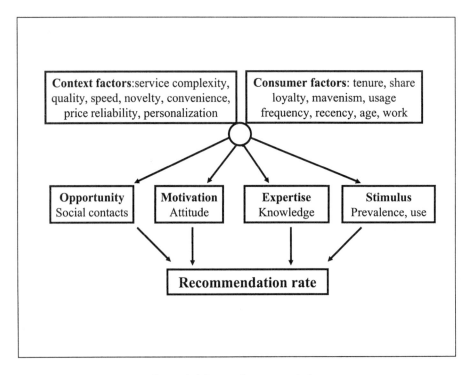

Figure 3.6. Bases of recommendation

How Long Do Advertising Effects Last?

Decay in the effect produced by advertising should not be confused with wearout. Wearout is the loss of ad effectiveness with repetition, i.e. the loss in the power of ads to influence consumers in the first place. Decay of effect occurs when the propensity to buy, or adstock (Broadbent 1984, see box), which has been generated by effective advertising, declines over time. This decay process will affect both the primary and the carryover effects of advertising. Figure 3.7 illustrates how, after a burst of advertising, these two decaying components may add to base sales. In Figure 3.7, the carryover effect is computed as an outcome of the primary effect. Figure 3.7 shows the combined sales effect (top line) as the sum of the base rate, primary effect and carryover effect.

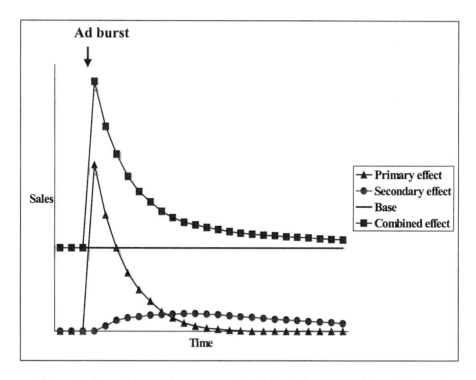

Figure 3.7. How primary and carryover effects of advertising may combine with base sales

---

Adstock

Adstock (Broadbent 1984) is a useful concept for thinking about the impact of past advertising. Adstock is the residual effect of the advertising for a brand that is left within people. Adstock is raised by ad exposure and reduced by forgetting and interference effects from other advertising. Forgetting shows an approximately exponential pattern of decay like that of radioactivity; i.e. the rate of decay is constant but, since it applies to a dwindling quantity, the change in the whole becomes less and less as it approaches some base level. Such processes are usually described by their half-life, the period of time required for activity to decay to half its original level.

Half-Lives in Frequent-Purchase Markets

Accurate estimates of ad decay are difficult to make because ad effects are relatively weak compared to the sales variations produced by price promotions for the brand and its competitors. Despite this, a number of studies have tried to estimate adstock half-lives. These estimates were based on the assumption that there was a single process of decay rather than two effects, each with different half-life. On this basis, Broadbent (1984) claimed that, for most brands, half-lives are in the region of 4-6 weeks and some cases in the *Advertising Works* series report half-lives of this order, e.g. four weeks for Oxo and twelve weeks for Andrex (Baker 1993). A meta-study of 70 brands by Clarke (1976) indicated half-lives in the range 4-12 weeks, with 90 percent of the ad effect exhausted within nine months.

Which Day Should You Advertise?

1. Suppose that a product is only sold on one day of the week. Sunday newspapers are an example. Which day should you advertise? Obviously as near as possible before Sunday, so Saturday if advertising costs are the same each day. But, if ad costs on Saturday are more than 4.4% (the daily ad decay rate) above those on Friday, it may pay to advertise on Friday.

2. Groceries have an uneven pattern of purchase over the week. Spending is heavier on Thursday, Friday and Saturday when compared with Sunday, Monday, Tuesday and Wednesday. The Nielsen (2003) figures are shown below:

Weekly supermarket expenditure by day of the week (% of total)

Monday	Tuesday	Wednesday	Thursday	Friday	Saturday	Sunday
12.0	10.7	12.0	16.1	19.7	20.9	8.7

This suggests that better returns will be obtained from an exposure if it goes out on Wednesday or Thursday evening rather than Saturday, Sunday or Monday evening.

Recent research has indicated that ad decay has both short-term and long-term components. Roberts (1999) found the aggregate short-term ad decay for a number of frequently purchased brands. This fitted an exponential curve with a half-life of only sixteen days and shows that, on average, an exposure loses 4.4 percent of its sales effect each day and 72 percent after 28 days. This rapid loss of effect has practical implications (see box) and also casts doubt on the earlier work showing longer decay periods.

Long-Term Decay Effects

Figure 3.7 illustrates a small long-term effect, which rises and then slowly decays. This slow decline is probably because the advertising of competitors gradually weakens allegiance to the focal brand. Without competitive advertising it is likely that sales would be relatively constant since, in these conditions, habitual behavior would be undisturbed. Evidence gathered by IRI on upweight tests is relevant to long-term decay (Lodish and Lubetkin 1992). In this study, the brands had been in the market for at least a year and the upweights were 50-100 percent in the test year only. Approximately half of the weight tests on 44 brands showed a sales increase in the test year. Lodish and Lubetkin analyzed the extra sales for these brands and compared results with consumers who had not received extra advertising. Table 3.3 shows the extra sales in the upweight group over three years.

Table 3.3. Percentage Sales Gain in Upweight Group (Lodish and Lubetkin 1992)

	Test year %	Year 2 %	Year 3 %
Sales gain	22	14	7

Table 3.3 demonstrates that the extra sales that occurred in years 2 and 3, after the upweight had finished, were roughly equal to the extra sales during the test year. This work was criticized for excluding unsuccessful weight tests that might have shown a response in later years but Lodish et al. (1995b) showed, using a sample of thirteen brands, that there was no such later response. Lodish et al. also showed that advertising raised both penetration (the percentage of people buying) and purchase frequency (the mean number of purchases made by buyers) in the upweight year but that gains in the following year were mostly due to purchase frequency, i.e. extra purchases were being made by existing buyers rather than by new buyers.

Lodish and Lubetkin (1992) show that some of the sales effect from advertising can persist for a long time. Roberts (2000) has also studied the effect of advertising over a longer period. He divided customers into those who had, and those who had not, been exposed to advertising for grocery brands in the previous 28 days. The analysis took account of weight of viewing, concurrent promotions and brand size. Repeat purchase of the brand in the subsequent twelve months was higher if the ad had been seen. Roberts assessed the extra sales in the year as 5.6 times the short-term increase in sales. When these extra sales are taken into account, advertising will often pay off over a year. Agencies are now estimating the long-term effect from advertising; Millward Brown International claims to show a large long-term benefit (Hanssens, Parsons and Schultz 2001, p.59).

Broadbent and Fry (1995) proposed a *floating base* model to explain how ad effects persist. In their account, there is a short-term effect that rapidly decays and a base sales level. The base sales level is not constant but moves up and down in response to different forces. There is a downward force from the marketing support for other brands and, counteracting this, there is an effect from ad exposures. Broadbent and Fry found that their model performed better than one in which a single decay process was postulated. Since the sales performance of one brand depends in part on the ads for other brands, the model could be developed to assess advertising in the whole category.

Conflicting Evidence on the Decay of Ad Effect

Econometric estimates, though varied, have suggested that most ad effect is rapidly dissipated. In a review of econometric studies, Leone (1995) found that, on average, 90% of the ad effect was realized after 6-9 months. A similar conclusion was reached by Mela, Gupta and Lehmann (1997). The IRI experimental work by Lodish and Lubetkin (1992) indicates a considerably longer period of effect from advertising. Some distortion in the measured duration of the sales effect may be due to the way in which data are aggregated by year in the case of the IRI findings but the results are too discrepant from earlier research for this explanation to be sufficient. The discrepancy seems to relate to the assumption of a single decay process in econometric modeling. If sales decay has both a short-term component and a second long-term component, the discrepancy may be resolved.

Segments to Target

It is easy to point out that, to be effective, advertising should concentrate on those who are most responsive. The difficult part is to identify the responsive segments and to find ways of reaching them at low cost. This means that we need to know how different audience segments vary in their general responsiveness to ads. Below, we consider three audience characteristics that relate to TV advertising: viewing level, loyalty, and weight of purchase of the advertised brand.

Heavy and Light Television Viewers

Heavy viewers are less sensitive to television ads. Roberts (1999) divided households into the 40 percent with the lightest viewing pattern and the rest. When he compared these light and heavy viewers, the light viewers had over twice the sales response of the heavy viewers. Roberts suggests that the greater responsiveness of light viewers is a 'share-of-mind' effect; i.e. the light viewer experiences less clutter so that the ads that are seen have more effect. Another reason for their greater response is that light viewers get fewer exposures and therefore wearout should be delayed for them.

Light viewers tend to watch at peak time (6.00pm to 10.30pm in Britain).

The combination of light and heavy viewers creates the peak. Roberts compared off-peak-only and peak-only viewers and showed that peak-only viewers had three times the sales response of the off-peak-only viewers.

Loyalty Segments

A study by Tellis (1988) on one mature product category showed that ads had more volume effect on buyers who were loyal to the advertised brand (measured as share-of-category requirement (SCR) greater than 50 percent) [1]. Those who had not bought the brand before showed only a small volume sales response to the advertising compared with loyal buyers. Before Tellis, Raj (1982) had found that those with an SCR loyalty of between 50 and 70 percent showed most sales response to advertising. One explanation for the lesser response of the very loyal (above 70 percent) is that these buyers have fewer other-brand purchases to switch to the focal brand. However, Raj found that the purchases of other brands were not much affected when the focal brand gained; in his study, the extra sales in the 50-70 percent loyalty group came mainly from an increase in category purchase.

Roberts (1999) reports that the low-loyalty segment (SCR less than 10 percent) shows the greatest, and the high-loyalty group (SCR more than 50 percent) the least, *percentage* increase in sales per buyer (Figure 3.8). This evidence appears to differ from the findings of Tellis and Raj, but this is not so. The latter researchers were concerned with volume increase, not percentage increase, as measured by Roberts. In Figure 3.8 the increases are on different bases for each histogram because the high-loyalty customers buy more of the brand than the low-loyalty customers. If we make the crude assumptions that all loyalty groups buy the same amount of the *category* and that average loyalty in each segment is the mid-point of the band, we find the incremental volumes per buyer shown in Figure 3.9. Here we see that the largest volume increase occurs for high-loyalty buyers. If our crude assumptions are roughly correct, Roberts' evidence is thus similar to that of Raj (1982) and Tellis (1988) [2].

However, the large number of consumers in the low-loyalty segment complicates this issue. Although the volume per individual low-loyalty buyer may be modest, the aggregate gain in volume from *all* low-loyalty buyers can be very substantial when compared with the gain from the smaller number of buyers in the high-loyalty segment. Figure 3.10 shows the sales impacts per segment assuming the numbers per segment given in another study (Baldinger and Rubinson 1996). From this analysis we conclude that aggregate sales gains come mostly from the large number of low loyalty buyers.

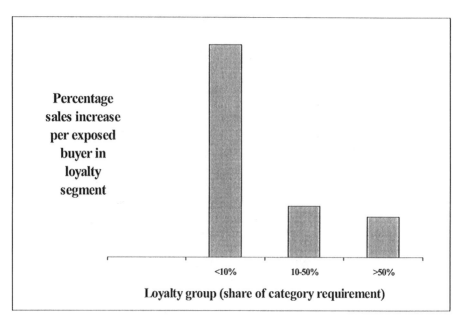

Figure 3.8. Percentage sales effect of advertising by customer's loyalty group

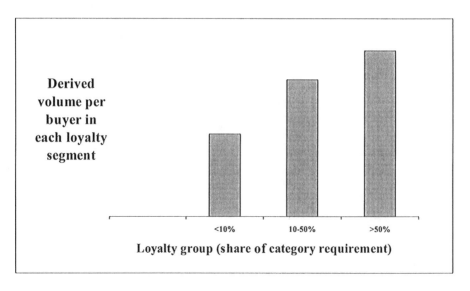

Figure 3.9. Volume sales effects of ads per loyalty group (derived from Roberts 1998)

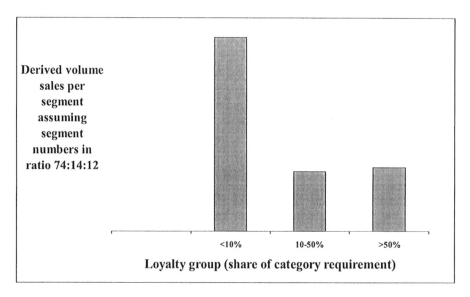

Figure 3.10. Total volume sales per loyalty segment (derived from Roberts 1998)

This evidence helps us to understand the *rather different roles performed by one-to-one direct marketing and media advertising.* The former, using sales force, mail, and telephone in conjunction with a database, allows the supplier to target the best buyers economically while the latter provides access to the large number of low-loyalty buyers and non-buyers from which a number of more loyal buyers may eventually be derived. When promotion is only directed at the existing customer base, the development of customer loyalty in the low-loyalty segment is not well addressed. This issue is given relevance by reports of reduced media spending by companies that have developed loyalty schemes. Our analysis indicates that media spend and loyalty support have different outcomes and that a sound marketing strategy may employ both of them.

Heavy and Light Buyers

We can describe markets in terms of penetration (the percentage of people buying in a given period) and purchase frequency (the mean number of purchases made by buyers in that period). Heavy buyers have greater purchase frequency. The distribution of purchase frequencies of a sample of buyers follows a gamma distribution (Ehrenberg 1988). Figure 3.11 shows gamma distributions for two brands with high and low mean frequencies of purchase respectively. In both cases, there are many light buyers and few heavy buyers but the heavy buyers are responsible for a large part of the total sales. In quarterly or yearly data, the distribution of sales usually fits a *heavy-half rule*: the heavy 50 percent of buyers is responsible for 80 percent of the sales. The ratio becomes more extreme as the period taken for analysis increases. This is because a longer period captures a higher proportion of light buyers. Over a period of several years, the pattern is closer to the 80:20 rule, i.e. 80 percent of the sales come from the heaviest 20 percent of buyers.

When a brand gains sales, which may be as a result of advertising, the increase occurs mainly in the light buyer segment. Over short periods we see this more as an increase in penetration, i.e. more buyers. This occurs because those who buy occasionally, but who did not buy in the reference period, now buy in the growth period and swell the penetration. If the reference period is longer, most of these occasional buyers are captured in the reference period so that growth is now manifested mainly as an increase in purchase frequency. However, in both cases the fundamental effect is the same: sales growth comes principally from the light buyer segment[3]. This is similar to the loyalty segment evidence, discussed above, that growth comes mainly from the large number of low-loyalty buyers. Indeed, there will be some overlap in these effects since low-loyalty buyers are often light brand buyers.

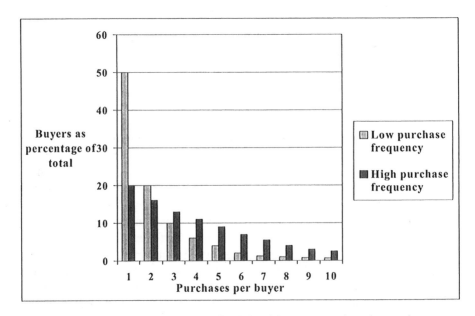

Figure 3.11. Gamma distributions for high and low mean purchase frequencies

Do Some Brands Get More From Their Advertising?

Big Brands

Big brands have somewhat greater purchase frequencies than small brands but considerably higher penetrations; thus brands are big mainly because they have more buyers rather than because each buyer buys them more frequently (Ehrenberg 1988). If the sales response from advertising depends mainly on the number of buyers, big brands will get more total volume uplift from an ad campaign, other things being equal. But the evidence often shows stronger gains for smaller brands. Big brands may be near their penetration ceiling so that much of their advertising serves to retain buyers rather than to increase sales. Long established small brands can have a large number of past buyers who may be activated by advertising. Also, the advertising of small brands is often infrequent and this may make it more effective when it does occur. An example of this could have been the successful Co-operative Society advertising campaign reported by Broadbent (2000); here, an old and relatively small store brand, which was very well known and had not advertised for some time, did very well when it returned to advertising. Another study by Riskey (1997) found that ads for small brands were more likely to deliver significant volume increases than ads for big brands. This may have been partly because the small brand ads tended to report some advance in the brand and these 'newsy' ads were more effective.

In summary, although big brands usually have more buyers, a small brand may get a good response from advertising if it has not advertised for a while, has something new to say, and has a long history.

New Brands

One type of brand that inevitably starts small is a new brand. Despite this, new brands are often introduced by advertising. But then, what alternative is there? Unless the new brand can be directly marketed, it must use media advertising to let potential customers know that it exists. One comfort here is that the ad elasticity is high for new brands. Advertising elasticity is the ratio of the proportional increase in sales to proportional increase in advertising. Lodish *et al.* (1995a) found an elasticity of 0.05 for established brands and 0.26 for new brands. Care must be taken when comparing these figures. The novelty of a product may help it to gain attention but, even though a new brand shows a high elasticity, the gain in volume can still be modest because base sales are few. Furthermore, buyers of new brands may not stay. They are willing to try new brands and so may move later to yet newer brands.

Elastic Categories

In some fields the boundaries between categories have little meaning to buyers. Consumers may replace Coca-Cola with beer and butter may displace margarine, as shown by the Lurpak case in Broadbent (2000). Thus, an increase in consumption of one brand may occur at the expense of other brands in the category *and* brands outside the category. As a result the whole category can grow and individual brand sales may be more responsive to advertising. Sometimes the sales taken from other categories can benefit the whole category; for example, in South Africa, Pampers expanded the whole disposable diaper market when they increased advertising (Broadbent 2000). Because of gains from other categories, food and drink brands are particularly responsive to advertising in comparison to toiletries and cleaners where brands can only gain at the expense of other brands in the category. Supporting this effect, unpublished Unilever research showed greater ad response among food and drink categories than among cleaning and toiletry products. However, the greater ad response of food and drink brands must have its reverse side since, in these fields, gains in sales can be whittled away by same-category competitors *and* by brands in other categories.

Summary

At some point an ad should be replaced by new copy but there is little agreement about the speed of ad **wearout** or the mechanisms involved, despite the losses that must be incurred when worn out advertising is used. Part of the problem here is that we lack a model of ad effect that includes the effect of repeated exposure. A model is proposed in which ads may have two sorts of **primary** effect: one is **thoughtful**, and quite strong; the other is **automatic**, passive, and weak. Thoughtful processes occur early in the sequence of ad exposures if they occur at all; automatic mechanisms can occur at each exposure so ads can continue to have some effect for a long period.

When primary effects occur there are likely to be consequential **carryover** effects that include **framing** (persisting change in thinking about the brand), **purchase reinforcement** (later purchase is increased by the occurrence of the earlier purchase), better **distribution, recommendation,** and **emulation.**

Models of advertising effect show better results when it is assumed that ads have short and long-term effects that decay at different rates. In one study, the short-term component had an average half-life of 16 days. The long-term component can persist for a year or more after the advertising has finished.

In the response to television advertising, more sales increase comes from **light** viewers than **heavy** viewers. The latter suffer from more clutter and *earlier wearout. When the response to advertising is examined as a function of **loyalty**, the more loyal users show more volume gain per user. However, because there are many more low-loyalty users of a brand than high-loyalty users, advertising will usually show more total volume gain in the low-loyalty segment. Similarly, when advertising response is examined in relation to a buyer's **weight of purchase**, a larger proportion of total gain comes from the large number of light buyers rather than from the relatively few heavy buyers.*

It is not clear whether big brands or small brands benefit most from advertising. Small brands have shown large gains, which may be connected to the novelty and rarity of their advertising.

New brands usually have to advertise on launch. Their measured advertising elasticities are much greater than those for established brands but these figures are computed on small base sales. As a result, advertising may not deliver much volume to the new brand.

Notes

1. Share-of-category requirement means the share of category purchases devoted to the focal brand.

2. These are crude assumptions. The low-loyalty group includes people who do not buy the brand and the high-loyalty group includes some 100% loyal buyers who are often light buyers.

3. There will also be some genuinely new buyers who have not bought before, particularly when the product is relatively new in the market and has a growing customer base.

Chapter 4
HOW DO INDIVIDUALS PROCESS ADVERTISING?

We now examine theories that have been used to explain how people attend to and process advertising. We look first at traditional sequential models such as AIDA. These models define some necessary requirements for ads to work but the causal relationships that have been claimed on their behalf are often in doubt. The ATR (awareness, trial, reinforcement) model is a better description of how advertising functions but also gives a limited explanation of the processes that are involved in effective advertising.

Turning to these processes, we examine first those that relate to attention and then those that are more concerned with processing. We assess the evidence for a number of mechanisms that could provide an automatic response to advertising and describe the Elaboration Likelihood Model, which provides an explanation of how people shift between conscious thought and automatic mechanisms.

Hierarchical Models of Ad Response

Traditionally, the influence of advertising has been explained as a hierarchical sequence of effects, passing from attention to the ad through to action, usually purchase. Strong (1925) attributed the earliest of these sequential models, AIDA, to St Elmo Lewis (late 19th Century). Figure 4.1 illustrates AIDA and the more extended model proposed by Lavidge and Steiner (1961).

Colley (1961) also claimed that there was a sequential process underlying ad effect and proposed the DAGMAR (**D**efining **A**dvertising **G**oals and **M**easuring **A**dvertising **R**esults) procedure for developing and assessing advertising. According to Colley, effective advertising took the audience down the path of **A**wareness, **C**omprehension and **C**onviction to **A**ction (ACCA), see Figure 4.2.

Hierarchical models deal only with the individual response and leave out any carryover effects of advertising (reviewed in Chapter 3). These models have some affinity with the social psychological work of the Yale School, which focused on the effects of different communication designs. In Yale

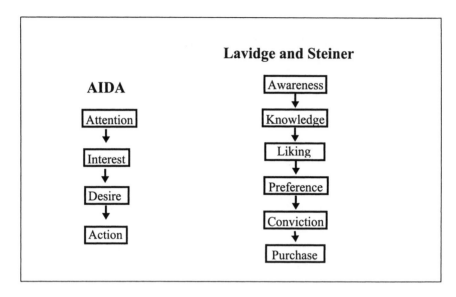

Figure 4.1. Hierarchical models of ad response

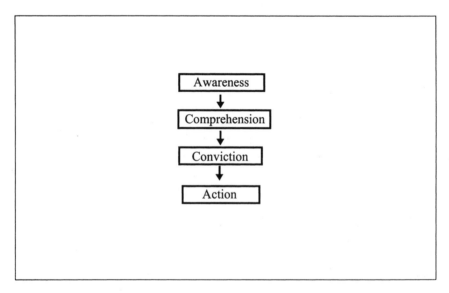

Figure 4.2. The model behind DAGMAR

research, different message elements were compared, their order was varied, and the endorsement of experts was manipulated. The Yale work was developed and popularized by McGuire (1968), who saw the persuasion process as a chain; if one of the links of the chain was broken the transmission of the message failed and persuasion could not occur.

There is a chain when ads work. Ads need *exposure*, some consumer *attention to* and *processing of* the ad, and they must leave a *residual effect* in the consumer that may affect a later purchase decision. But, in addition to these necessary connections, there may be causal links between exposure, attention, processing and buying propensity that must be investigated empirically. Do people need to remember the ad in order for it to affect their behavior? Do they need to understand what the ad is about? Below, we examine these connections in more detail.

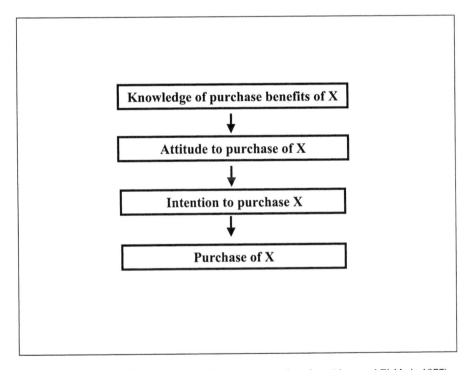

Figure 4.3. A compatible sequence leading to purchase (based on Ajzen and Fishbein 1977)

We start by looking at the larger picture, the whole hierarchy. At this level, we have good reason for doubting whether a strong sequence of effect will be found because measures at the top of the sequence (awareness of the advertising, understanding the message) are not *compatible* with measures at the bottom of the hierarchy such as intention to buy the brand and actual purchase of it. By compatible we mean 'specified in the same way'. Ajzen (pronounced eye-zen) and Fishbein's (1977) work on the link between attitude and behavior has demonstrated that an attitude measure designed to predict behavior must be compatible with the behavior measure if the prediction is to be strong. For example, Ajzen and Fishbein point out that the use of oral contraception is well predicted by the attitude to *using oral contraception* and only weakly predicted by the less specific attitude to birth control. This is because the use of oral contraceptives is associated with a number of consequences (effectiveness, convenience, safety, side effects) that are taken into account in the attitude to using oral contraceptives. The more general attitude to birth control may not include these consequences. Applying this thinking to hierarchical models, awareness of the ad, and even awareness of the brand, does not necessarily connect with the consequences of buying the brand. A more appropriate sequence, which is based on Ajzen and Fishbein's idea of compatibility, is shown in Figure 4.3.

The Awareness-Trial-Reinforcement (ATR) Model

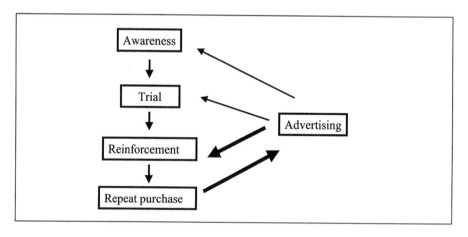

Figure 4.4. The Awareness, Trial, Reinforcement (ATR) model (Ehrenberg 1974)

In established markets, ads act mostly on those who are already buying the brand. Since these consumers already know and understand the brand, the stages of sequential models that deal with attention and recognition are largely redundant. Instead, ads serve to reinforce the existing pattern of behavior. Terms such as *reminding* (McDonald 1992) and *nudging* (Barnard and Ehrenberg 1997) are used to explain the function of advertising when the product is already familiar. This was the position taken by Ehrenberg (1974) in the Awareness-Trial-Reinforcement (ATR) model. In this description of ad function, shown in Figure 4.4, the main effect (heavy arrows) is to confirm existing purchase patterns.

In new markets, awareness and trial may have to be built up in order to gain new customers but, in established markets, ads mainly retain customers. So, except in new markets, Ehrenberg (1974) rejects the idea that advertising works mainly by acquiring new customers for the brand in order to make up for those that have defected. He describes this as the *leaky bucket theory* of advertising (Figure 4.5). In this theory, advertising maintains the level in the brand bucket by converting buyers of other brands and by conscripting non-buyers of the category. The leaky bucket theory gives advertising a *strong* offensive role in the battle to maintain share. Ehrenberg offers instead a *weak* defensive theory of advertising. In his account, buyers rarely change their brands and ads serve mainly to reinforce existing purchase tendencies. Ehrenberg's views have been supported by Tellis' work (1988), which showed that advertising served mainly to confirm preference for currently bought brands rather than to stimulate switching.

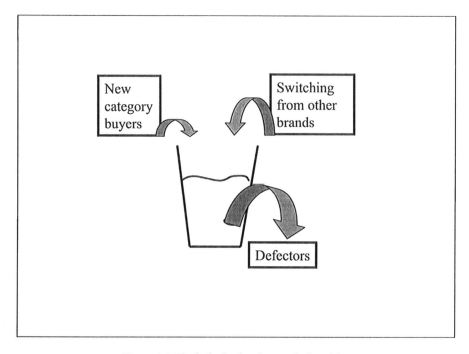

Figure 4.5. The leaky bucket theory of advertising

Ehrenberg (1974) suggests that a number of processes may be involved in defensive advertising. As noted earlier, selective attention may operate so that people notice more easily the ads for the brands that they buy. He also points out that ads help consumers to see the benefits that they derive from their brand purchase – a framing process. Such framing is likely to encourage repurchase of regularly bought goods and services. In the case of durables, where repeat purchase is infrequent, it may make the buyer a better advocate of the brand. Ehrenberg has revisited this work in further papers (see Barnard and Ehrenberg 1997, and Ehrenberg 1998).

Conversion or Reinforcement
The strapline 'No FT, no comment' has become familiar to British audiences. It tells them that those who do not read the Financial Times are poorly informed and ill equipped to deal with business life at the higher levels. This ad may convert some readers of other papers but it also reinforces current readers of the FT by telling them that they are wise to read the paper and are well informed as a result. In fact, it is not in the interest of the FT management to recruit too widely because, if they dilute their readership too much, ad rates could fall.

One claimed effect of advertising after purchase is to give reassurance to buyers. Those with *insufficient justification* for their choice may feel a negative state of arousal called *cognitive dissonance* and may seek out supportive information (Brehm and Cohen 1962). High-cost items are thought to need more justification and may therefore create this arousal more often than low-value items. Advertising, although clearly biased, may provide some reassurance. But consumers are often elated rather than worried by the products that they buy and it is probably this *positive* arousal rather than dissonance that makes them receptive to any relevant information. Unease about a major choice seems quite rare; in one study of car purchase, only two percent of buyers found the choice difficult (Pearce 2000).

No Role for Conversion?

Even when overall sales show little change, markets can contain a quite large buyer churn – the bucket does leak a bit and new converts keep it topped up. In established grocery markets, East and Hammond (1996) found that about 15% of buyers defected from their favorite brand each year and were replaced by about the same percentage of new buyers. This suggests that advertising may sometimes acquire customers. Most customer acquisition occurs because a consumer has switched from another brand but some acquired customers are new to the category, and have often entered a life stage that requires the category. Categories that are bought for relatively short periods, e.g. disposable diapers, have high proportions of such new entrants and this makes recruitment in these cases substantial (see box).

Customer Acquisition Rates

What are the approximate annual acquisition rates of new-to-the-category customers in two different markets: washing powder and disposable diapers? Assume that these markets do not show overall gains and losses.

Suppose that consumers start buying washing powder when they are 20 and stop when they are 70 years old. This would give a 50-year period as customers. Every year, 2% will leave and be replaced by a new 2% if the overall market does not change. Now consider the diaper market. If women have two children and use disposable diapers until their children are 2 years old, their average buying period would be 4 years (ignoring the case when the second child is within 2 years of the first). Thus, in a market with no overall change, 25 percent would leave each year and would need to be replaced by the same percentage of new recruits.

The idea that ads work mainly to reinforce existing purchase patterns may be seen as particularly suited to grocery categories where repeat purchase continues for long durations. But even in durable markets, reinforcement can occur since most durable purchases are replacements or additional purchases (Wilkie and Dickson 1985, Bayus 1991). In the car market, cars are exchanged at intervals of about four years and repeat-purchase rates of 30-70 percent have been reported (Ehrenberg and Pouilleau 1991). This leaves scope for brand shares to grow if repeat purchase increases. But a substantial increase in a durable brand's share cannot be explained in this way if it occurs over a relatively short period. Cases in the *Advertising Works* series do sometimes show gains that are too large to be explained as the outcome of improved retention, e.g. the 61 percent increase in Volkswagen sales in the UK from 1994 to 1997 (Kendall 1999); such cases indicate that some ad-induced conversion has taken place.

Attention to the Ad

Pre-Attention Processing

The environment offers many objects for examination and a subconscious process is required to select objects for attention. Janiszewski (1988) investigated whether this pre-attention process could affect the evaluation of an object, even when the object was not selected for conscious processing. The study indicated that later evaluation of a stimulus was raised by exposure to the stimulus, even when it could not be recalled and was therefore unlikely to have been consciously processed. This means that the response to brands may be changed without the respondent being aware of the influences that produced the change. Unconscious processing of this sort may be responsible for a significant part of ad effect.

Conceptual Conflict

The first exposure of an ad is likely to secure more attention because we alert to unusual stimuli. People give more attention to objects that are novel, changing, incongruous, surprising, complex or indistinct (Berlyne 1954). Such objects are salient in the sense that they command attention and people make a cognitive effort in order to understand them. Sometimes, understanding is delayed, either because there is no easily accessible frame of reference by which to interpret the stimulus, or because there are more frames than one and it takes time to choose between them. Berlyne described the state induced by such stimuli as *conceptual conflict.*

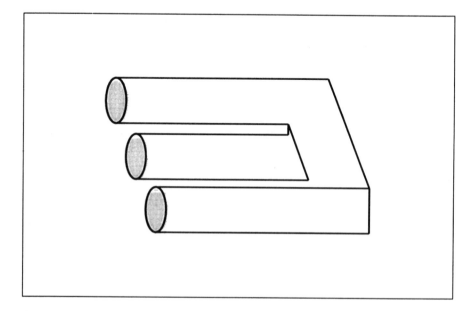

Figure 4.6. Blivet MkIV

When people are exposed to a stimulus that creates conceptual conflict they may resolve the conflict so that further exposures arouse little attention, but some stimuli, such as Blivet MkIV (Figure 4.6), may be impossible to resolve. This diagram plays on the perceptual mechanisms that we use for making three-dimensional sense from two-dimensional information and holds attention because there is no reconciliation possible between the diagram and our three-dimensional experience.

Some ads may arrest attention because they create conceptual conflict. The Wonderbra campaign, discussed earlier, probably did this. It used billboards for the ads, which was an unusual medium for bra advertising. The woman portrayed was enigmatic, provocative and non-submissive, which was an unexpected combination for an ad. The phrases used were not easy to place and could give rise to discussion about who had said them in which film.

Salience

In everyday usage, objects are described as salient when they stand out and draw attention. Guido (2001) argues that salience is not just a feature of the stimulus but arises from an interaction between the stimulus characteristics and the receiver's ideas in a specific context. As a result, some stimuli arrest the attention of some people but may leave others unaffected. This helps to explain how ads can differ in effectiveness between cultures.

We are used to the idea that salient stimuli may draw our attention but, in another sense, salient stimuli are those that are easily and quickly apprehended in preference to others. Guido's *dichotic theory of salience* recognizes these two different forms. *In-salience* is the term used to describe the attention-drawing stimulus that is contextually incongruent with the receiver's ideas, and *re-salience* is used to describe the stimulus that is contextually congruent with the receiver's ideas. Advertising can contain both types of salience and the familiar re-salient component may work with the in-salient component to increase the 'take' from the ad. For example, an ad in a teen magazine that is designed to raise contraceptive use among males might show a pregnant man (in-salient) together with a discussion about how to avoid pregnancy (re-salient). You can see similar elements in the smoking pregnant nude ad (Figure 4.7). The use of familiar ideas is discussed later under the heading 'Archetypes'.

Really successful ads do not just raise attention. Attention is required, but attention to what? The skilled copywriter makes the resolution of any conceptual conflict dependent on the understanding of the ad message. Often,

Figure 4.7. Saatchi and Saatchi poster combating smoking when pregnant
(Crown Copyright, reproduced by permission of the Health Development Agency)

a sexual component in the ad draws attention but this must be relevant to the message so that any resolution of conflict raises the significance of the product. For example, the Wonderbra is designed to enhance breast cleavage and this was well expressed in the ads. Another example of effective use of sexual content occurred in an ad designed to discourage pregnant women from smoking (Figure 4.7). The nudity emphasizes both the pregnancy and the smoking and this helps to focus attention on the message.

Selective Attention by Buyers of the Advertised Brand

Because of need or relevance, those who use a brand are more likely to perceive ads for that brand. People often find that, after buying a new product, they notice the ads for the product more. This helps to explain why advertising has more impact on existing users, as claimed by Ehrenberg (1974).

Rice and Bennett (1998) showed that both awareness and liking of ads were higher if those seeing the ad were users of the brand. Figure 4.8 shows that the awareness of Brand A ads is higher among users of Brand A and the awareness of Brand B ads is similarly higher for users of Brand B. This effect probably depends upon the increased cognitive accessibility of brands that are used. Stapel (2000) presented similar evidence. He compared claimed ad recall by loyal buyers and others. Table 4.1 shows the results for beverages in the Netherlands. The loyal buyers recall the ads for their preferred brands better than other people do.

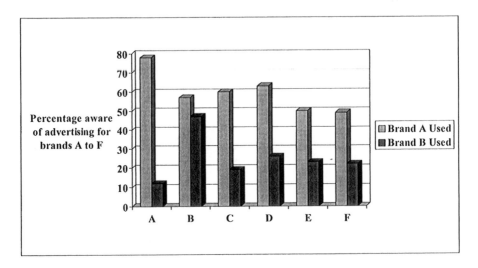

Figure 4.8. Awareness of brand advertising and brand use (Rice and Bennett 1998)

Table 4.1. Claimed Ad Recall (Stapel 2000)

Beverage	Loyal buyers %	All others %
Heineken	54	39
Coca-Cola	41	24
Grolsch	37	15
Pepsi Cola	32	20
Bavaria	23	12
Mean	**37**	**22**

Ad Processing

Archetypes

Although novelty attracts attention, it also causes conceptual conflict, which slows down processing. By contrast, the use of familiar (re-salient) elements in ads may raise processing speed and can be used to deliver more information or more subtle distinctions of meaning. This focuses interest on the way in which well known frames of reference can be used to aid perception and thought. Lannon and Cooper (1983) showed how many ads make use of culturally shared meanings in order to engage the audience and impart ideas. Such cultural forms or *archetypes* might include the beer drinking working-class male, Father Christmas, the 'new man', the busy mother, the go-getting businessman, the 'anorak', and the waxed-jacketed English countryperson.

A related idea is to be found in the thinking of Jeremy Bullmore (1998). He explained how advertising has to engage the audience so that people *converse* with the ad. To do this, the ad must fall within the range of interest of the audience so that people can think in the terms of the ad. This means the ad must have components that they find familiar. For advertising practitioners these issues are central to the nature of effective advertising. Ads and their audiences should *not* fit Rebecca West's rather arch observation that *"there are no conversations, only intersecting monologues"*.

Conversation with ads may be assisted when ads use familiar archetypes, or, more generally, familiar schemata. A schema is a generalized knowledge structure that is stored in memory and archetypes are one type of schema. People use schemata to make sense of their environment, to link different phenomena and to infer consequences from a given stimulus. When information is limited, schemata may be used to work out what is missing.

In marketing, the schema is often the category. Usually, the category is well established and the advertising effort is devoted to adjusting the position of the brand within this category. But sometimes, particularly in the area of food and drink, the category is uncertain. Is Horlicks a nourishing drink that anyone can enjoy or is only for the elderly? Are alcopops to be regarded as alcoholic drinks, which they are, or are they to be seen as alternatives to fruit juices and colas, which they are too? Mostly, ads do not question the normal classification of a brand but sometimes it is necessary to contest assumptions and to try to re-position a brand in a different category. One example is the way in which health advertising needs to present the consumption of cigarettes as a cause of disease and premature death, and thus oppose the idea that they are an acceptable personal habit.

The problem of an unfamiliar schema is demonstrated in Figure 4.9. The left-hand form is often seen incorrectly as a picture frame when it is briefly presented. Those who do woodwork can recognize it as two try squares. If the try-square schema is primed first, as on the right, the diagram is more likely to be seen correctly. This helps to explain why some really new products may take time to become accepted. People may just lack the cognitive structures that are required to understand the product and it is hard to create these structures with advertising. It is better if the new product can be shown as an extension of an existing idea.

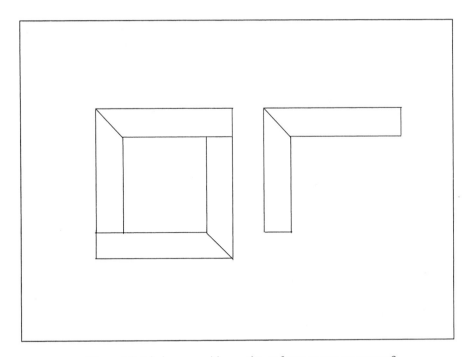

Figure 4.9. Priming recognition: a picture frame or two try squares?

Advertising Awareness and Understanding

Does advertising awareness relate to the sales effectiveness of a campaign? Channon (1985) observed that the advertising for Cadbury's Fudge was very effective on sales but it had little effect on ad awareness. Broadbent and Colman (1986) found little relationship between ad awareness and sales effectiveness in a study of eighteen campaigns in the confectionery market. Other work on ad recall showed no evidence that it is related to the sales impact indicated by copy tests (Lodish *et al.* 1995a). We conclude that ad awareness need not be related to ad effectiveness.

Does comprehension of the ad assist its effect? It is argued that the message in an ad must be understood if it is to be effective. It seems likely that ads that are incomprehensible will not have much effect under most circumstances. Certainly, agencies do not like using an ad that is not understood (see box).

Checking Ad Understanding

One example of poor understanding occurred in the development of the advertising for the Clio car in the UK (Baker 1993). The campaign was based on a French father and daughter discreetly conducting their liaisons with the aid of their Clio cars. Originally, it was intended to use more French language in the ads but the agency, Publicis, found that the British audience could not understand this. As a result, the first ads contained only two words in French, *Papa* and *Nicole*. A later ad used *Maman*. Without this simplification, the campaign might have been less effective though other campaigns have used un-translated terms, e.g. Audi's *Vorsprung durch Technik.*

Attitude to the Brand

Does attitude to the brand affect purchase? In a study of the buyers of 27 brands, Baldinger and Rubinson (1996) interviewed over 4000 consumers. They divided buyers into high, medium and low-loyalty segments using share-of-category requirement ranges of below 10 percent, 10-50 percent and over 50 percent. A year later, 56 percent of the sample responded when they were re-contacted. In both the first and the second surveys, the interviewees were distributed across the three loyalty ranges, high, medium and low, in the percentages: 74, 14, and 12. This apparent stability concealed substantial movement of customers between the loyalty segments over the one-year interval, much more movement than the investigators expected[1]. However, these changes in loyalty were partly a product of the low numbers in the higher-loyalty segments; chance effects can make small segments less stable.

The researchers measured attitude to the brand in the first survey and found that this predicted some of the change in behavioral loyalty. If the attitude toward the brand was more positive than the initial behavioral loyalty would imply, there was more chance of a switch to greater loyalty and, if the attitude was less positive than the initial behavioral loyalty implied, there was more chance of a reduction in loyalty. However, these effects were quite weak. Ehrenberg (1997) criticized this paper and the authors responded with a summary of their thinking (Baldinger and Rubinson 1997).

Attitude to the Ad

A study by Haley and Baldinger (1991) showed that a small sample of successful ads scored more highly on liking for the ad compared with unsuccessful ads. But, because the researchers worked backwards from success in this study, it had little *predictive* value. However, the view has gained ground that attitude to the ad (A_{ad}) predicts ad effectiveness. One way this could happen is that ads that are liked make the brand more liked (A_b), and this leads to more purchase behavior (B), or summarily $A_{ad} \rightarrow A_b \rightarrow B$.

This raises a problem of causal order. Does attitude A_{ad} affect A_b, as suggested, or vice versa? There is evidence that attitude to the brand may *follow* purchase in grocery markets (Dall 'Olmo Riley, Ehrenberg, Castleberry, Barwise, and Barnard 1997); this brand liking could then make the advertising for the brand liked. This reverses the causality, i.e. $B \rightarrow A_b \rightarrow A_{ad}$. Although this sequence is plausible, it is widely assumed that the causal process is from A_{ad} to A_b and thence to purchase. In a sophisticated analysis, Madden and Ajzen (1991) examined both paths, i.e. whether A_{ad} affects A_b, and whether A_b affects A_{ad}. Their work indicated that only the $A_b \rightarrow A_{ad}$ path was significant. This surprising finding casts doubt on whether attractive advertising changes attitude to the brand and, by extension, purchase of the brand. Madden and Ajzen could only test a limited set of conditions and it is possible that the $A_{ad} \rightarrow A_b$ path will be supported under other circumstances. But, against the claim that A_{ad} builds A_b, it should be noted that there are cases where an ad is disliked but is nonetheless effective, for example, advertising for Charmin toilet tissue in the United States and the Radion advertising in Britain (Feldwick, 1991). If $A_{ad} \rightarrow A_b$, this would not be expected.

Strong claims for A_{ad} are made by du Plessis (1998). He suggests that ads that do not arouse some emotional charge will not be processed. Du Plessis (1994) showed an association between message recall and the likeability of the message but, as we have seen, recall is not a satisfactory criterion of ad effectiveness. Undermining du Plessis' claim about the effect of emotional charge is evidence that the salience of a stimulus depends more on the *cognitive* than the *affective* disturbance it creates (e.g. Blivet Mk IV, earlier).

Research on the effect of emotionally arousing advertising was conducted by Ambler and Burne (1999). They used beta-blockers to reduce emotional arousal in subjects. According to their theory, this would reduce processing so that less recall and recognition would be found when these subjects were compared with controls. This is what they did find and they concluded that the affective response to an ad tends to increase processing and to enhance recall of the ad. However, it is possible that the beta-blockers had other effects beside inhibition of affect and that these other effects altered processing or recall. Ambler and Burne's paper relates to a more general model of advertising proposed by Vakratsas and Ambler (1999). In this model, the ad processing response is assumed to tend to inertia; this inertia is counteracted by the originality of the ads and the respondent's involvement in the category which may combine to shift the receiver first to affective processing and then sometimes to cognitive processing.

The Effect of Mere Exposure

This was studied by Zajonc (pronounced Zi-onse) and Rajecki (1969). They investigated the evaluation of meaningless words, symbols and photographs of unknown persons when these were exposed at different frequencies under experimental and naturalistic conditions. Figure 4.10 shows how evaluation increased when exposures were presented under laboratory conditions. Similar effects were observed when the exposures took the form of ad-like entries in the student newspaper.

The explanation for the mere exposure effect has been contentious but it seems likely that it arises from a reduction in conceptual conflict. Initially, respondents will have no appropriate schema for interpreting a nonsense word but, with repetition, some sense is given to the stimulus. The reduction in conceptual conflict is rewarding and this reward value is transferred to the stimulus as increased liking. Bornstein (1989) criticized this work and questioned whether it was relevant to advertising. However, Zajonc and Rajecki also used field studies in which the nonsense words were presented in a similar manner to ads and this diminishes the criticism.

Mere exposure has been related to ad effect by Batra and Ray (1983). In their work, the exposures were realistically presented under simulated clutter conditions. They found that repeated exposures did increase evaluation although the manifestation of this effect was delayed. Batra and Ray suggested that mere exposure was involved in ad effect but they also argued that frequency of exposure lifted brand salience so that the brand was more readily recalled and recognized.

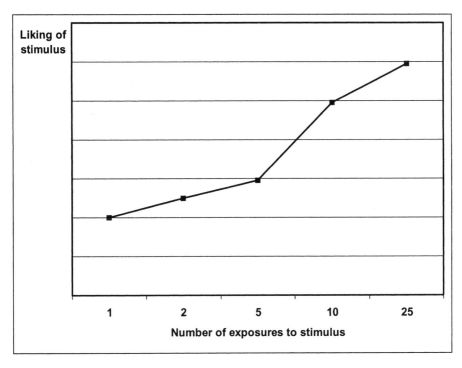

Figure 4.10. Composite results from mere exposure laboratory research (Zajonc and Rajecki 1969)

Positive and Negative Information

Mizerski (1982), Wright (1974), and others have found that negative information has more impact than positive information on the beliefs of consumers, and Fiske (1980) found that negative information drew more attention than positive information. Wilson and Peterson (1989) reviewed word-of-mouth research and found that, generally, instances of negative word of mouth had more effect than those of positive word of mouth. However, negative information about a brand is often resisted if consumers are already committed to the brand (Ahluwalia *et al.* 2000). This corroborates a finding by Wilson and Peterson (1989) that information is only accepted about a brand if it is congruent with the consumer's attitude to the brand. From this work we conclude that negative ads will have most impact when a product is new and unfamiliar to purchasers, or when consumers have already decided to abandon one brand and are looking for another.

The greater impact of negative information is widely accepted and one public relations practice treats negative comment as having four times the weight of positive information (the Merriam formula, Kroloff 1988). One reason why negative information has more impact is that it is rare. Fiske and Taylor (1991) noted that people say more positive than negative things about others. Also, in free markets, products do not easily survive if they cause dissatisfaction. When most information is positive, negative information is more surprising and draws attention when it is encountered (Fiske 1980).

Evidence that negative information has more impact than positive information might suggest that it should be used in advertising to attack competitors. Indeed, this is commonly done in political advertising. But a feature of political choice is that there are often few realistic options. In a choice between two alternatives, negative information that eliminates one alternative settles the matter. But, when there are many brands to choose from, positive information about one brand that puts it ahead may have more effect than negative information about another brand that eliminates only that brand. Another problem with negative advertising is the finding, previously noted, that prior brand commitments may inoculate an audience against negative information. Also, predominantly negative advertising may cause distaste and encourage an audience to avoid the advertised category entirely.

Heath's Work

Low-involvement processing of ads has been discussed in papers by Heath (2000a, 2000b) and now more extensively in a book (Heath 2001). Heath argues that brand choice is not usually based on a rational assessment of the brand but rather on 'markers' created by emotional experience or learning. Heath claims that advertising, except when read as text, is mostly handled passively and responded to subconsciously. According to Heath, this implicit learning is not analyzed or interpreted but takes place automatically and without awareness. The ad is retained in chunks, and the holistic way jingles can be recalled on cue supports Heath's account. Heath suggests that ads that are stored in this way are quite durable when compared with more active learning.

According to Heath, ads do not have much effect on markers when they are taken in but the repeated processing of implicit learning at low attention levels leads to the gradual establishment of 'meaningful' associations with the brand that then affect brand choice. Thus markers develop through the interaction of stored ads and experience.

But if there is little processing when the ads are received, how can they be stored in a coherent manner? Memory is organized and new information has to be stored within this memory organization. Some processing seems to be required in order to define the location of new information in memory just as some knowledge of a book's content is required if it is to be placed correctly in a library.

Heath offers a general theory of low-involvement response to ads but he does not address issues that should be covered by such a general theory; these issues include the effect of repeated exposures, the nature of wearout, short and long-term decay of effect, and loyalty segment differences. Heath also argues that the low-involvement nature of ad processing means that methods of pre-testing such as the ARS Persuasion Measure are inappropriate since they will pitch the respondent into a high-involvement response to the ad, which is not how people react to advertising on most occasions. But, contrary to this, Blair and her colleagues show that the ARS Persuasion Measure is very effective (Blair and Rabuck 1998, see box).

Persuasion Measures of Ad Effectiveness
In ad effectiveness research, persuasion is a shift in the propensity to purchase. Such shifts are used as a proxy for buying when testing ads. Early measures of persuasion were developed by the Schwerin Corporation in the United States. Subsequently, the Research System Corporation, which absorbed the Schwerin organization, developed a standardized test called the *ARS Persuasion Measure*.

The ARS Persuasion Measure is based on the shift in brand choice from before to after ad exposure. This is obtained in a secure, off-air, simulated purchase environment (Jones and Blair 1996). 120 respondents, aged 16 or more, are used per ad. Despite the somewhat artificial conditions, a report by Blair (1987) indicated that the test did work. The soundness of Blair's analysis was then questioned, first in an Advertising Research Foundation Workshop paper and then in a review by Lodish *et al.* (1995a). The reader should understand that Blair is the president of the Research System Corporation and Lodish is closely associated with IRI. Ad testing is a major interest of both companies and the Research System Corporation test is quicker and cheaper than that used by IRI.

Jones and Blair (1996) reported further supporting evidence, and criticized the IRI work. Lodish (1997) responded, defending his report. Blair and Rabuck (1998) then reported more studies of the link between sales and ARS scores. They found a correlation of 0.71 between ARS Persuasion scores and short-term market performance. In this study there were no controls for ad weight, price, promotions, coupons, or competitor activity, which makes the correlation all the more impressive. It appears that quite a strong indication of effectiveness is obtained when advertising is assessed at an early stage using the ARS methodology, but this controversy may not be over yet. Ad testing is reviewed in more detail by Rossiter and Percy (1997).

In other respects one may agree with Heath. For example, he points out how low-involvement advertising can affect preference without any recall of the advertising. This is to be expected if the advertising is absorbed with little processing. Heath has stimulated interest in low-involvement response but his account contains some unresolved problems.

Psychological Research on Persuasion

There are some differences of emphasis between psychological studies of persuasion and ad research. In particular, psychological studies often pick fields that elicit high involvement, such as health decisions, whereas much advertising, especially on television, deals with products of limited interest to the recipient. For this reason, securing attention to ads has more importance in advertising research. Even so, the psychological research on persuasion should have some relevance to advertising effects[2].

Arguing with the Ad

When the topic has interest or relevance to the recipient, initial reactions to a persuasive message are likely to be thoughtful. Sometimes, these responses may support the message, i.e. they are *pro-arguments*. More often, the recipient will argue against the message and reject it. This phenomenon of *counter-arguing* was used to explain why messages could be more persuasive when subjects were distracted (Festinger and Maccoby 1964). A study by Osterhouse and Brock (1970) showed that, as distraction increased, counter-arguments fell and persuasion in the direction of the message was greater. In these studies, the persuasive message contained low-quality arguments to which an attentive subject might easily make objection. The role of cognitive responses was further supported in a study by Petty, Wells and Brock (1976) who showed that, when the predominant response was to agree with a well-constructed persuasive message, distraction reduced the number of pro-arguments and slightly reduced persuasion.

In an experiment that could relate to effective frequency, Cacioppo and Petty (1979b) required student subjects to listen once, three times, or five times to well-constructed arguments about increasing university revenue. As the frequency moved from one to three, subjects were more persuaded and generated positive arguments for the proposed change. The further increase in frequency from three to five reversed these effects. Cacioppo and Petty argued that two processes were at work. At first, elaboration of the message occurs as pro-arguments are introduced but then, with more repetition, tedium cuts in and this motivates subjects to counter-argue and reject the message, despite its cogency. In a later study, Cacioppo and Petty (1985) conducted a similar experiment using poor quality arguments. In this case, as expected, the message acceptance declined when exposures were increased from one to three. This was probably because the poor quality message generated counter-arguments from the start. These studies suggest that better arguments stand more repetition. But in advertising research a reverse position is sometimes taken. This is that people quickly 'get the point' with a well-constructed message so that less repetition is needed (Batra and Ray 1983).

Silencing Counter-Arguments

Responses to a message tend to take one of four forms (Petty and Cacioppo 1986b). These are: source derogation, counter-arguments, pro-arguments, and curiosity statements. With this in mind, it may pay to include elements in an ad that enable positive responses and curtail negative responses. For example, the strong credentials of a source can be implied and pro-arguments may be assisted by including facts in the ad that could be used in such arguments.

A campaign to recruit police officers in Britain used the theme "I couldn't. Could you?" after showing realistically unpleasant work that has to be done by the police (Rimini 2003). This apparently negative approach was remarkably successful and it was estimated that 6000 extra police officers were recruited via this advertising. One reason why the ads may have worked is that they may have silenced negative counter-arguments and possibly promoted pro-arguments.

Cacioppo and Petty (1979a, 1979b) also relate persuasion to the respondent's involvement in the issue. In one study, involvement was varied by manipulating whether or not the respondent was directly affected by a proposed administrative change. They found that increased involvement amplified the dominant response: when the message generated pro-arguments, there was more persuasion; when counter-arguments were generated, there was less persuasion. However, a review of the effect of involvement by Johnson and Eagly (1989) showed that when the message was weak there was no consistent effect.

The Elaboration Likelihood Model (ELM)

The ELM is an extension of the cognitive response model discussed above. Petty and Cacioppo (1981, 1986a, 1986b) argue that persuasion takes place by two routes: the *central route* and the *peripheral route*. The central route is concerned with the assessment of arguments and the cognitive response to them. The peripheral route employs more automatic mechanisms such as heuristic (rule-of-thumb) methods, as well as mere exposure and simple association. Psychologists have tended to give most attention to central processing and claim that this is likely to produce a more long-lasting change. In advertising research, there is more focus on the peripheral route since people have little time to deal with the many ads that they see each day and conscious assessment is likely to be rare and confined to the first few exposures if it occurs at all.

The Elaboration Likelihood Model. Summarized Postulates
(Adapted from Petty and Cacioppo 1986b)

1. People want to hold correct attitudes.

2. But elaborate thinking about issues is limited by the context and by individual characteristics.

3. Contextual influences include content that can form part of a persuasive argument, can act as a cue to peripheral mechanisms, and may switch the receiver's response from one route to the other.

4. Objective assessment may be modified by variables that affect motivation and the ability to process.

5. As elaboration is reduced, peripheral cues become more influential, and vice versa; this means that the two forms of processing compete for mind-space.

6. Contextual and individual factors can bias or inhibit processing so that inferences are biased.

7. Attitudes that are produced by central processing will be more resistant to change and more related to behavior.

Petty and Cacioppo (1986b) express the model as seven postulates about elaboration likelihood, which are summarized in the box. A key part of the ELM model, as its name implies, is the likelihood that the respondent will process a stimulus via the central route. There are three considerations here:

- *First*, well-argued elements in a message can directly facilitate central processing. For example, the information that *"most of those who die in fires asphyxiate while they are asleep"* may be used to direct thinking about installing smoke alarms.
- *Second*, aspects of the message, e.g. its length or the accent of the actor delivering it, may set off mechanisms that stop central processing and switch on peripheral processing. For example, a long message may elicit the *'length implies soundness'* heuristic and different accents may have associations that affect the evaluation of the message (a German accent in

an Audi ad could enhance the attitude to this product but might do little for a fragrance).

▪ *Third*, the message elements can alter either the motivation or the ability to elaborate. Distraction, as discussed above, will reduce the likelihood of elaborate processing. Personal relevance will increase it.

Elaborate processing does not mean that any conclusions are validly inferred or accurate. Distorted conclusions may occur because elements in the message bias the objectivity of processing. In objective processing, message elements may allow a person to focus on key points and flaws. In biased processing, elements may produce a focus on irrelevant factors, or may distract a person from relevant factors.

Heuristic Mechanisms
A heuristic mechanism is a simple response that uses only part of the information available. These mechanisms are learned. Examples are:
▪ More readily recalled information is more probable (the availability heuristic)
▪ Longer arguments are more reliable (length implies strength)
▪ Experts can be trusted
▪ If people agree they are probably correct (the consensus fallacy)

The ELM, with its central and peripheral routes, corresponds with the thoughtful and automatic processes in the model of advertising effect proposed in Chapter 3. However, the ELM model presents central and peripheral processes as alternatives whereas the model in Chapter 3 allows them to occur concurrently. The division into central and peripheral processing has some similarity with Fazio's (1990) MODE model in which behavior is either guided automatically via mechanisms or more consciously by deliberate processes. Fazio treats these as alternatives but some evidence shows that they are interrelated. A study by Baldwin and Holmes (1987) showed that deliberate responses could be systematically affected by the requirement to visualize certain persons before responding. This visualization seemed to induce automatic mechanisms that favored certain conscious responses. One conclusion from this work is that all thought involves automatic mechanisms, which sometimes lead to conscious reasoning. The *heuristic-systematic model* (Chaiken, Liberman, and Eagly 1989) allows concurrent central and peripheral processing and is discussed by Eagly and Chaiken (1993).

Summary

Hierarchical models have some truth since ads cannot have any effect unless people are exposed to them, and then process them to some degree, but some empirically testable links have not been supported.

In Ehrenberg's Awareness-Trial-Reinforcement (ATR) model, ads for established products serve mainly to retain existing buyers who selectively perceive ads for products that they use.

*There is evidence that ads can have an influence even when they are not consciously noticed; this occurs because some automatic pre-attention appraisal is required **before** a stimulus is selected for attention and this appraisal can leave effects. When people do attend to stimuli, including ads, it is often because the meaning of the stimulus is uncertain or unusual, which causes conceptual conflict. Familiar information may cause little conscious attention but it is quickly understood and can assist the rapid transfer of ideas. Negative information usually has more impact than positive information and this may be because it is unusual.*

It has been proposed that well-liked ads are processed more than ads that arouse no feeling, that there is some transfer of affect from a liked ad to the brand, and that attitude to the brand will predict later switching. However, the evidence for these proposals is weak.

In psychology, the Elaboration Likelihood Model (ELM) specifies two paths for influence. Communications either cause a thoughtful or an automatic response. The elaborate process involves pro and counter-arguing while the automatic response uses heuristics and association.

Notes

1. Among the low-loyalty buyers, 87% remained in the low-loyalty segment (9% moving to the medium-loyalty and 4% to the high-loyalty segments). Among the medium-loyalty buyers 33% remained in this segment with 47% moving to the low-loyalty group and 20% to the high-loyalty group. Among the high-loyalty buyers 53% remained in the high-loyalty segment with 25% transferring to the medium-loyalty group and 23% to the low-loyalty group.

2. Eagly and Chaiken (1993), particularly Chapters 6 and 7, give a more detailed account of the psychological research on persuasion.

Chapter 5
ADVERTISING AT THE POINT OF SALE

Most media ads work indirectly since they are received in one location but the purchase occurs later in another location. This means that the purchase context should revive the ad effect and the ad content should help this process. But when ads are delivered at the point of purchase, there may be a substantial impact on sales because action can occur immediately before any decay of effect. We see this in stores when discounts produce large sales increases and we consider whether the signaling of a discount should be seen as a form of advertising.

The point of purchase can contain more than one method of promoting the brand and we report evidence on how two or more methods can work together.

The Chapter is divided as follows. First, we consider how media ads may have their effect rekindled at the point of purchase. Second, we explain briefly the current evidence and thinking on the response to advertised price changes. Third, we review the evidence on the relative effects of discount, store display, and local advertising. Fourth, we look at experimental evidence on the sales impact of an additional display in a store.

Display Effects

Many influences occur at the point of purchase (POP). Beside the goods in the shops we see discount notices and special displays that are designed to affect our current behavior. Outside the purchase context, we receive many 'point-of-performance' instructions and admonitions, e.g. to switch off mobile phones or to observe speed restrictions. These instructions may be described in a variety of ways but, as attempts to influence our behavior, they may be likened to advertising; we will call all such point-of-performance or point-of-purchase material *display*. There is little systematic research on display effects. This is partly because the point of purchase usually falls outside the control of manufacturers and their advertising agencies.

It is clear that the presentation of goods and any accompanying notices can focus attention and arouse interest. We want to know how such displays affect behavior and we consider three functions that they may have. One function of display is to *relate to media advertising* so that the effect of this past advertising is revived. A second function is to *affect buying directly*, whether or not there is any related media advertising. A third function of display is to *work with other point-of-purchase* factors, such as discounts, to produce enhanced effects. We need to know whether the effect of each component of the promotional mix *adds to* or *multiplies* the effect of other components.

The Delayed Effect Of Advertising

Reviving the Ad Effect

Ads can arouse a propensity to buy, which may result in purchase or other action when conditions permit. Sometimes, ads set a person on a consciously chosen course of action that results in purchase. This is particularly relevant to high-involvement purchases such as a smoke alarm. Domestic fires usually kill by asphyxiating people in their sleep. Advertising can explain how smoke alarms awaken people before it is too late (Baker 1995). This could create a conscious intention to buy an alarm. More commonly, the effect of ads is less consciously experienced. As Broadbent (2000) puts it, shops sell, ads predispose. When the brand is already familiar, an ad may raise its salience, making it more likely that it is the brand that is recognized or recalled on cue. The ad may also attach more value to the brand so that it is preferred to other brands in the category. A further function of the ad is to establish links between the brand and various needs, objects, and symbols, so that the brand is brought to mind when these other factors are encountered, often in buying contexts.

The packaging of groceries and the fascias of retail outlets are the most important links between ad and purchase context. When the brand is a good, the colors, pack shape, and name act as cues to purchase. Seeing a brand on the shelves may remind customers about their need and may cause them to recall some benefit of the brand that has been presented in advertising. Holden and Lutz (1992) point to several other brand and advertising cues that may be illustrated in the purchase context. These include brand benefits, the product category and even competitive brands: seeing Surf may remind a customer to buy Tide if this is their regular brand. Advertising should be designed to strengthen the associations between the brand and important cues. Many ads deliberately include features that are found at the point of sale.

Figure 5.1 shows the sort of associations that might get customers to think of buying Coca-Cola. Some of these cannot be used in ads for Coca-Cola, e.g. Pepsi, or vodka when advertising to children, and a short list is required of those that can be employed. From these, advertisers may emphasize those that can be used in both ads and specific purchase situations.

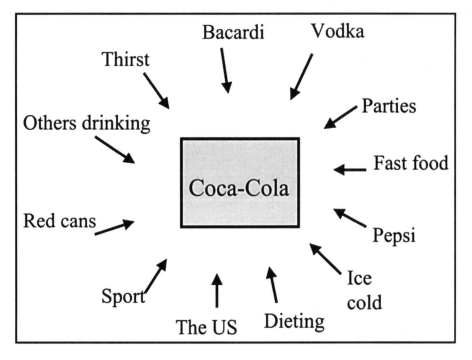

Figure 5.1. Possible links to Coca-Cola

Making Connections

When agencies are considering ad copy, a useful exercise is to construct a diagram like the one above. What are your diagrams for Virgin, McDonalds, or holidaying in Australia or the Netherlands? Which of these associations could be used in advertising?

A more systematic technique for gathering associations is called *laddering*. In this process, consumers are asked a series of questions designed to link their values to product attributes via a means-end chain. The resulting map shows the routes whereby a product may fulfill consumer needs. Those who follow this procedure then seek to show in the resultant advertising how the consumption of the product will satisfy consumer needs and values. A problem with this approach is that it assumes a rather rational model of ad effect. See Gutman (1982) for more on laddering.

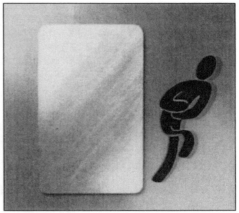

Figure 5.2. Ads for Imodium (by permission of The Campaign Palace, Australia)

Sometimes, imaginative brand naming and advertising capitalizes on everyday features of the environment. By incorporating these into the ad, the brand is called to mind whenever the environmental feature is encountered. In Australia, the male lavatory symbol (known as the *dunny boy*) was used in ads for Imodium, a treatment for diarrhea (*Effective Advertising 5*, 2000). Just seeing the dunny boy symbol could remind people of the product, particularly if they were in need of it. Ads were placed, appropriately, on the back of toilet doors in airports.

Mood Management

Mood states are pervasive but relatively temporary conditions, which may raise interest in products that relate to the mood. We are familiar with some mood associations that have been established by social convention. For example, champagne is associated with celebration, elation and achievement. Ads may capitalize on such associations or may try to create them. Ads for Coca-Cola seek to present the brand in the context of social warmth. Some ads for children's foods feature the mutual appreciation of parent and child. If we accept that particular moods are associated with particular products or types of product, it follows, as suggested by Gardner (1985), that retail contexts that can evoke these moods by point-of-purchase display and décor may help customers to remember relevant brands.

The generation of mood in the retail context is the field of *atmospherics*. This is the management of the store interior, particularly its color, space, sound, aromas and décor to induce specific mood responses and behavior.

Donovan, Rossiter, Marcoolyn and Nesdale (1994) have suggested that the store interior should evoke both pleasure and activation. If customers find the environment pleasant, they are likely to stay longer. If the store is activating, customers may be stimulated to interact with staff and buy goods. But, although consumer response can be observed, it is difficult to show that this is caused by mood, and that any mood is caused by the store interior. Milliman (1982) found that the tempo of music in a supermarket affected the speed of customers through the store. When the tempo was slow, they took more time and bought more. This could have occurred because the music affected their mood but, alternatively, their behavior might have been directly cued by the music.

In one study, the observed effect does not seem to be attributable just to mood. North, Hargreaves and McKendrick (1997) played background music in a wine store. When French accordion music was played, French wine outsold German wine, and when German beer cellar music was played, the German wine outsold the French. The music origin seemed to directly cue wine choice. Customers were not aware of this influence on their behavior. However, mood remains a likely facilitator for many types of purchase, and ads that harness a brand to the relevant mood are likely to have more effect.

Types of Purchase Context

There are obviously many different purchase contexts but one distinction is particularly important. In many contexts, brand awareness occurs as *recognition*, usually by sight but sometimes through hearing or smell. In this case, an awareness of need follows rather than precedes brand awareness. In self-service stores, the usual process is recognition. Rossiter and Percy (1997) point out that when this applies, ads should present the brand before the need. In other contexts, where the brand is not present, need occurs first and *recall* is then required. For example, you might realize that you need a haircut and this causes you to remember your hairdresser. Recall is particularly relevant to services, which are usually cued by need.

Recognition and recall dictate different media choices. Visual recognition is served well by television, posters, and magazines because the brand can be pictured. Brand name recall is assisted by radio when the brand is represented more often as a name than as a visual form, as is usually the case with services. Only when the product is mainly heard, e.g. music products, is radio suitable for recognition. Other media, such as the Internet, can serve both recall and recognition.

The Rossiter-Percy Communication Model

The Rossiter-Percy communication model (Figure 5.3) pulls together some of the issues considered at different points in this book, including the distinction made above between recognition and recall. The idea here is to match ad type to the type of purchase decision. An early approach of this sort, the FCB grid, divided product purchase decisions by asking two questions: is the purchase primarily a matter of feeling or thinking, and is the purchase high or low-involvement?

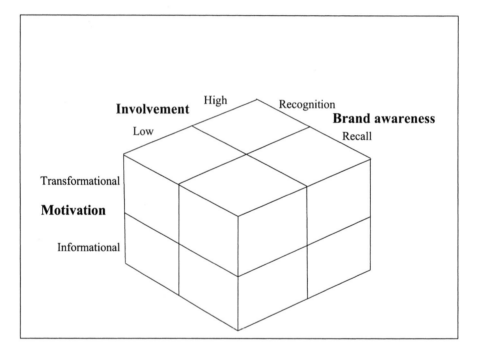

Figure 5.3. The Rossiter-Percy octants

Rossiter and Percy (1997) extended the FCB grid. *First*, they distinguish between the modes of brand awareness, whether via recall or recognition. *Second*, they retained the involvement dimension in the FCB Grid and noted that this often distinguishes first-time purchases (where the buyer must be recruited) from those for whom purchase has become routine (where the buyer must be retained). *Third*, Rossiter and Percy replaced the thinking-feeling dimension with an informational versus transformational motivational dimension; here, informational products such as aspirin are instrumental to other purposes and lack intrinsic value, while transformational products such as flowers and music are intrinsically valued. Some products can fulfill both purposes; for example, a pair of Nike trainers gives good support for the feet as well as being a fashion statement in some consumer segments.

The Response to Price

The way in which price is regarded by researchers has been slowly changing. Economists used to present price as a hazard that deterred purchase but this does not address the mechanisms that are invoked when a consumer assesses price. In consumer behavior, research on price has been based on the idea that prices are judged against a price reference or expectation. When questioned, people will report an expected price and Briesch, Lakshman, Tridib and Raj (1997) found that these reports were predictable from a weighted average of prices recently paid.

Early research on price knowledge examined the accuracy of price recall in the grocery field. Gabor and Granger (1961) found that about 70 percent of UK housewives could report the exact price paid. This was at a time when most consumers were poor, prices were regulated to be the same in every store, and there were far fewer brands. Later, with more wealth, price deregulation and more brands, accurate recall of price dropped. In the United States, Dickson and Sawyer (1990) found that only 47 percent of shoppers could give the price of the item that they had just put into their shopping trolley. In France, Vanhuele and Drèze (2002) found that, if shoppers were asked about price as they entered the store, the proportion knowing the exact price was only 2 percent, though 19 percent of shoppers were within 5 percent of the true price. This evidence undermines assumptions about price: how could the price be judged against an internal reference price when shoppers have so little knowledge of the correct price?

Vanhuele and Drèze address this problem. They argue that consumers know price in different ways and exact recall of price is quite rare. What is more important is whether consumers can recognize bargains or overpriced goods, when these are presented. They conducted a study using 5 percent and 20 percent increases and decreases in price, relative to the normal price. The researchers concluded that customers were mostly poor at detecting whether 5 percent variations were bargains or not, but most people could recognize that a 20 percent discount was good value and a 20 percent over-price was bad value. Only about 14 percent of the sample were clueless and classified a 20 percent discount as bad value or a 20 percent over-price as good value. Vanhuele and Drèze conclude that, in the grocery field, price awareness is generally not accurate but that it can direct behavior toward cost saving if the variations from standard price are greater than about 10 percent. This work indicates that people engage in *implicit* price recognition; i.e. they can make appropriate judgments even though they may not have any anticipatory price expectation or conscious awareness of price.

There is some parallel here with ad effects. Earlier, we drew attention to the low-involvement response to ads when people are influenced by the ad even though they have little or no awareness of being influenced. Vanhuele and Drèze's work suggests that, similarly, people mostly respond to price differences without much awareness. We have also noted a high-involvement response to ads and we can find a parallel to this in cases of precise price awareness. Some people know the exact price range for the grade of gasoline that they use and may go to considerable trouble to buy this product at the lowest price.

The purpose of this review of price perception is partly to challenge the idea that price is a simple matter of information about a cost. Usually, customers do not seem to compute cost saving in a precise manner and appear to take in price information in much the same way that they take in advertising and other product information, as background knowledge that is difficult to recall but which may still affect their behavior. This suggests that display material on price will produce effects in much the same way as ads, i.e. success will depend on the size, design, and location of the display.

The response to price is conventionally measured as price elasticity, the ratio of proportionate sales increase to proportionate price discount. Price elasticities are often in the region of −2 (i.e. a price cut of 10 percent gives a sales rise of 20 percent) but if the effectiveness of price discounts depends on how well they are signaled, elasticities are also dependent on the prominence and design of the in-store price display.

Price elasticities vary by category, by the price structure of the market, particularly when relative prices are clearly seen (Scriven 1999), and by stage in the product life cycle (Simon 1979). Also Danaher and Brodie (2000) have presented evidence that high market concentration of the category, the storability of the product, and low market share of the brand are positively related to the magnitude of price elasticity. However, as we see below, some of the most dramatic effects on elasticity occur as a result of in-store display.

Local Advertising, Price Cuts and In-Store Display

The US market research firm, IRI (Information Resources Inc), has reported on the single and combined effects of sales discounts, local advertising and display in grocery stores (IRI 1989). They found that a price cut of 15 percent produced sales increases averaging 35 percent, giving a mean brand price elasticity of –2.3.

Figure 5.4 shows the way in which each component contributes to increased sales. Local ads raise the effect of a discount substantially and in-store display even more. The right-hand histogram stack suggests that the components work synergistically, i.e. that the total effect of the three components is greater than the sum of the single effects. But, although synergy *may* occur, this study cannot prove that it does. This is because the stores that run the triple promotion (discount, display and ads) may be better organized than the others and may do each promotional element better. To test for synergy we require an experiment in which like is compared with like.

One finding from the IRI research was that in-store promotion had much more impact on the sales of some categories than others. For example, sales of toilet paper increased several times more than sales of women's sanitary goods when local advertising, discount, and display were used together. This could relate to the fact that some goods are easier to display. Related to this, an Advertising Research Foundation study (ARF 2000) found that the best location for display varied with the type of good, e.g. carbonated beverages sold more when displayed on the floor of the store.

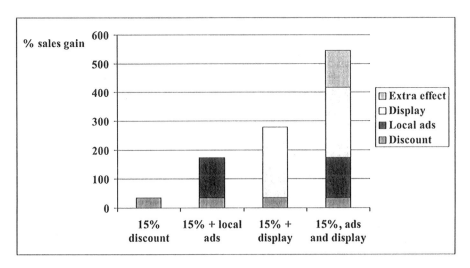

Figure 5.4. IRI evidence on the combination effects of price discount, display and local ads

Combining Displays

The IRI research findings need to be tested by experiment but there is no experimental study that compares the separate elements of the triple promotion with these elements in combination. However, some experimental evidence is available on adding an extra display in a store (East, Williamson and Eftichiadou 2003). What effect might be expected from such an extra display? If store displays are a form of advertising, we might expect them to work like ad exposures. A double display in the same store is like two ad exposures close together in time. As previously noted, most research has indicated that incremental exposures produce diminishing effects (Broadbent 1998; Jones 1995a; Roberts 1996; Simon and Arndt 1980) though there is some dissent from this position (e.g. Tellis 1988). But novel and complex products are expected to show initially accelerating sales with each exposure and Roberts (1999) has provided evidence that exposures that occur close together in time also produce this pattern. A response of this form indicates a form of synergy in which one exposure facilitates the effect of another. This evidence, coupled with the evidence from IRI above, suggests that two displays in the same store may produce more sales than two displays in different stores.

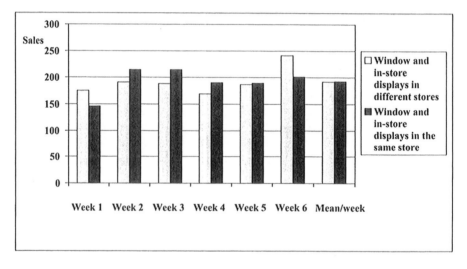

Figure 5.5. Display effects (East, Williamson and Eftichiadou 2003)

East *et al.* (2003) compared the sales from a window display and an in-store display in the same store (where synergy might occur) with the sales from these individual displays in different stores. The experiment employed 66 branches of the H. Samuel jewelry group in the United Kingdom and the displays featured G-Shock watches, a new brand developed by Casio. These watches were only on sale when displayed, so there was no background level of purchase. It can be seen from Figure 5.5 that the week-by-week comparisons show little difference between the two conditions. The overall means are much the same and indicate no synergy. This is interesting. The search for synergy has been a mantra in industry but, in this one case where a proper experimental design was employed, we find no synergy.

Case: Jeffrey Wallis

Jeffrey Wallis ran the UK chain of Wallis women's fashion shops for many years. He eventually sold the chain and then ran a number of Benetton shops. Over the years, he perfected a system for making the most of the display areas in the window and inside the store so that his Benetton shops recorded extraordinarily high levels of sales per square foot.

His system has the following elements:
- Use of dramatic solus displays, particularly of high fashion.
- Rotation of window displays over the day so that the different shopper segments passing during the day could be targeted with appropriate merchandise.
- Measurement of passing shoppers and those entering the shop so that the efficiency of the display in drawing customers could be measured.
- Measurement of purchases by those entering the shop so that the efficiency of the interior display and service could be assessed.

Fashion shops may be supported by media ads but their success depends heavily on their location, their merchandise selection and the display of this merchandise. Jeffrey Wallis' system, by providing objective measures of the effectiveness of display, gave managers the opportunity to experiment and to change displays that were not working well.

Summary

The purchase decision usually occurs in a different context to the one in which advertising is received. Purchase situations should therefore revive the effect of advertising that has been received earlier. To do this, they need to have factors in common with the advertising and ads should be designed so that they contain features of the purchase situation and evoke appropriate moods for the type of merchandise sold.

Some products, particularly service products, are bought because the context evokes the category need and the brand is then remembered, while other products, particularly groceries, are purchased because they are recognized and a need for the category is then remembered. Ad copy and media should be chosen to take account of the way in which a product is selected.

For the most part, people give a low-involvement response to price changes that parallels their response to advertising. Good or bad value is recognized if the price is sufficiently discrepant from the norm; value is not usually inferred from exact price knowledge. This casts doubt on the idea that people respond precisely to the information presented by a price notice.

Communication mix variables may work synergistically to produce more total effect than the sum of the effects of each variable on its own but one experimental study showed no evidence of synergy between two displays in the same store. More evidence is needed here.

Chapter 6
ONLINE ADVERTISING

Online advertising can support the brand in the same way as other advertising and can assist direct selling by precise matching of brand and consumer interest. We describe the methods of using the Internet and evidence on the effectiveness of this medium.

The Internet as an Ad Channel

Fascination and uncertainty have followed the evolution, and in many cases the demise, of Internet companies. For many of these companies, the financial return from Web-based advertising is key to their success or failure. Online advertising does have some special advantages and, to help us to assess these, we start by noting functions where the Web excels.

- Information transfer. Email is widely used. Internet users like the speed and efficiency of searches for information of all sorts.
- Booking. For example, hotel and travel booking can be done easily via the Internet.
- Market assessment. Alternatives can be compared; for example, prospective house purchasers can look at pictures of a house before deciding to visit. But although the Web allows easy price comparison, there may be loyalty to specific websites, and the technology of the Web (bookmarks, saved shopping lists) helps to reinforce this loyalty (Reichheld and Schefter 2000).
- Music, software, and other bit-based products can be downloaded.
- Gambling. The immediacy and lack of geographical constraint makes the Internet ideal for this.
- The purchase of technical products, particularly computers, since current users provide a good target group.

Using the Internet as a retail channel raises more problems when:

- The retailer is unknown and trust is lacking so that credit purchase may be compromised. Pornography, though very successful on the Web, has been associated with credit card scams, which may restrain growth in this sphere.
- A product is sold which has a physical form that must be transferred to the purchaser (clothes, groceries).

Social Influences

Zeff and Aronson (1999) have written an early but informative book about Web advertising, which describes the form of ads and the applications that are possible. Many studies focus on particular problems. For example, Hoffman and Novak (2000) address the problem of acquiring customers on the Web by using freelinks, partnerships and word of mouth. As a medium, the Web aids social influence (recommendation, emulation); this was estimated to contribute about 30% of customers in the case of one Internet firm, CD-Now.

Types of Internet Advertising

Ads on the Web can be banners (often sited at the top of the page, with a link to other sites), pop-ups, smaller buttons (a signaled link with minimal information), or 'interstitial' advertisements, which load behind other material and appear when other pages are cleared. Links can also be placed in the text. There are also public relations-type endorsements from interest groups and email messages about products to customers who have consented to receive them. Banners are mostly text and picture, which may be animated. Web ads are intrusive and there is evidence that they are disliked more than advertising in general (Schlosser, Shavitt and Kanfer 1999). But Web ads are more avoidable than those on media such as television because they can be deleted; indeed, slow-to-load ads may be erased at the frame stage.

Paying for Web Ads

Advertising on the Web cannot be assessed easily in terms of reach but, in some cases, technology is providing evidence of ad-related sales (see the box on EasyJet). To assess and pay for advertising, the usual Web measures are the number of impressions (as in the traditional print medium) or the number of clickthroughs (jumping to an advertised site). Flores (2000) points out that the repeated exposure of Web ads (without clickthrough) can build the brand in the same way as conventional advertising and the Web measurement firm, Engage (2001), estimated that a third of the effect of an online campaign may arise in this way. This makes the pricing of ads on the Web difficult; although Web metrics may permit charging per Web-based sale, this ignores the brand-building effect of Web ads.

When clickthroughs are used as the basis of ad purchase, site owners need to find the best fit between brand and page that will raise clickthroughs, while brand owners need to design ads and identify pages that will encourage clickthroughs from customers who then buy. This produces some difference of interest between site-owner and brand owner. Website owners want ads that raise clickthroughs while brand owners are wary of producing ads that get clicked by those who do not then buy. For example, if animation raises clickthrough without a corresponding increase in conversion, it may pay the brand owner to avoid animation in ads. Instead, a static banner can be placed on more pages. This focuses attention on the effectiveness of the different forms of online advertising.

Online Effectiveness

Flores (2001) reports that animated ads give double the clickthrough rate of static ads and that they also have a somewhat greater take-up among those who do clickthrough. Flores also found that copy differences were responsible for a substantial variation in sales response; thus, designing good copy is just as important with Web ads as it is with conventional advertising.

Swinfen-Green (2002a) has assessed the effectiveness of on-line ads. He claims that the brand-building effect occurs mainly on first exposure, not on clickthrough (which is rare) and argues that page impressions (exposures) should therefore be used to charge for advertising on the Web when brand-building is the primary purpose of the ads. Using awareness as a criterion of effect, he also notes evidence of a frequency effect: two exposures are markedly better than one but thereafter the effect builds slowly. In a second article, Swinfen-Green (2002b) compares banners, pop-ups, and superstitials. Pop-ups get five times the clickthough and twice the sales of banners but they have appreciable loading time and are often deleted at the frame stage when bandwidth is restricted. Superstitials do better than pop-ups since they are fully formed when seen and do not give the opportunity to delete when loading. Flores (2001) also examines the clickthrough rate as a function of ad file size; he finds that clickthrough increases with file size at first but then declines; this suggests that users often delete the slower ads. The wider use of broadband access, with its fast loading, may change the relative effectiveness of different types of ads.

Interest Matching

For a long time advertisers have tried to serve ads to appropriate interest segments. Some media, such as television, offer little scope for accurate targeting. By contrast, the Internet permits very accurate targeting because the ads that are served can be selected so that they relate to the receiver's particular interests when these can be established. Also, when customers agree to receive communications that are related to their interests, it is possible to be very specific, e.g. Amazon's emails to consenting customers.

For many mass-consumption products, precise targeting is of limited importance. Here, demographic criteria may provide an adequate guide to ad placement. But many other products are highly specific; for example flights to particular destinations, academic courses on particular subjects and jobs in particular fields. Specific products need to be matched to their small buying segment. This can be done by using *keywords*. In this respect the Web is like the trade press, but even more focused. A second technique for focusing on the interests of the website visitor takes advantage of the information held on Web users by Internet suppliers who use *cookies*. A third technique for improving the match of ad and visitor interest is to run *real-time studies* that test the effect of different ads or site designs. We now consider each of these interest-matching methods.

Internet Targeting

Try searching the FT.com site for business education. In practice, this means MBA providers. Which institution provides a banner ad? When I first tried, it was HEC in Paris. Now, others are there. On the FT.com site, someone who is interested in an MBA is easily presented with a major provider.

But the issue is more complicated for new products that are unknown and have uncertain associations. There is a software package for would-be novelists. If you know the name – *newnovelist* – it is easy to find with a search engine. What are the associations of this product and which of these might be searched for? Answers to these questions are needed if ads are to be placed on the Web to catch those who are not looking for such software but who might be interested in it.

Keywords and Key Sites

Suppose that you want to go to Bergen in Norway and you search for Bergen using an online directory or search engine. As you do this, a banner ad could appear offering you cheap flights to Bergen on Scandinavian Airlines. You have only to hyperlink to the SAS site or pick up the telephone and the transaction can be completed. In the winter, ads on last-minute Norwegian skiing opportunities could also do well on a Bergen site. This type of ad delivery is similar to the way Yellow Pages work. Search engine and directory output can be related to a large number of products with narrow appeal. Ingenuity is required to identify the right ad locations that capitalize on the reasons people have for visiting a website or searching for information.

Returns from different sites can vary widely as is shown by the EasyJet case (see box); this shows that, just as in offline advertising, targeting is most important.

EasyJet.com

EasyJet is a cut-price air carrier selling directly to the public via telephone and the Internet (with a small discount for using the Internet). A report on a Web advertising campaign was published in Broadbent (2000). The adspend was £100,000 and was distributed across eight sites. The best site (Excite) delivered a return on investment of 875 percent, the worst (Scotsman) 8 percent. Overall the Web advertising was clearly profitable and gave about 2.5 times the profit of telephone sales.

The study showed that:

- Getting the right site was very important. The best performing sites were (in order): Excite, AOL Travel, Cheapflights, Lycos.
- Clickthrough was an unreliable indicator of return on investment, partly because of differential conversion of clickthrough into sales. This supports evidence from Engage (2001) that there is often a mismatch between clickthrough rates and purchase.
- Forty percent of sales occurred on first visit. The remaining 60% of sales occurred, on average, five days later.
- After the advertising campaign ended, online sales dropped a little and then resumed their upward movement. It is not clear how much of this growth was due to growth in the online market, how much was bookmarking for later use, and how much was derived from recommendation from other users.
- The software used gave rapid feedback of effects to EasyJet so that adjustments to advertising were made daily by 'iFixers'. This is a role that may become automated as software develops (see Memetrics, below).
- In this case, the offline and online advertising seemed to have relatively independent effects on sales, so online gains were not at the expense of offline sales.

One of the most successful Internet companies is Google, the search engine site. It has low costs and does not need to advertise – its users tell others. It has more than half the search market and provides search services to many other sites. Ads on Google are all based on keywords. These take the form of simple text messages but Google works with major clients to sort out the most appropriate keywords. Businesses can also design their own ads and place them with Google online. Google claims a clickthrough rate of about 2.5 percent, ten times the level of many other sites. This superior performance seems likely to relate to the effective matching of interest via the keywords.

Cookies

A cookie is a small text file left on the user's computer as an indicator of a prior visit, which can be used by an Internet company to link a new visit to past visits and purchases. One company does not detect the cookies of another company and, because of this, firms like DoubleClick and Engage, act as the agent for many other companies, and are able to assemble detailed buying histories on visitors from cookies. The demographic criteria traditionally used for targeting are abandoned here in favor of past behavior, which provides an indicator of current interest. Without identifying the visitor by name or location, it is possible to select and serve an ad that is more relevant to the visitor's interests than one based on demographic criteria.

Real-Time Evaluation of Websites

A sophisticated technique for evaluating site effectiveness, including ads, is being developed by Memetrics.com. Part of the flow of visitors to a site is passed through an experimental design that compares the sales responses under different site formats. The sales effects are monitored and the site may be altered automatically to optimize business from the site (see box).

Memetrics.com

Established in 2000, Memetrics.com is the brainchild of Jordan Louviere, a marketing academic who has devoted much of his research energy to the application of experimental methods to marketing problems. Memetrics.com was set up to apply these methods automatically to website optimization. The technology identifies which features of a site (colors, placing, copy, pictures etc) raise sales or click-through to other sites and adjusts what visitors see in order to maximize profits from different user-groups.

An experiment involves the comparison of groups that are drawn on a random criterion. Each group receives a different experience. Memetrics can handle many different groups and assigns subjects to many different experimental conditions automatically. When enough visitors have been passed though the system, the analysis is conducted automatically and weights are computed for site features and for different classes of visitor. Then the site can be adjusted to take account of these weights.

Summary

The Web medium can be used to sell directly but also helps to build brand awareness in the same manner as conventional advertising. Online advertising can deliver widely different results so that improvements in copy and website placement offer large benefits. Narrow-interest products may be sold effectively if ads for them are placed so that they are served to Internet users with corresponding interests. These interests are revealed by search topics or by cookies that indicate past purchasing. The design of websites may be optimized by using automatic experiments that allows formats to be tested and modified in real time.

POSTSCRIPT

The interest in studying advertising effects is two-fold: on the one hand, explaining how ads work poses an intellectual problem of considerable difficulty; on the other, people may benefit financially if they understand how ads work and therefore how to use advertising effectively. The second outcome follows from mastering the first. Here, we review some of the new understanding of advertising that seems to be particularly related to financial benefit.

Advertising is a major business expense and reaches a double-digit percentage of turnover in many fields. In their perennial bouts of cost containment, firms sometimes slash advertising and promotion budgets. This results in some capricious changes in expenditure and the hunt is on for a more precise way of allocating spending on advertising. At one level this has been addressed; see for example Broadbent (1989) who painstakingly explains how to plan ad expenditure. But justifying advertising also requires an understanding of what it can and cannot achieve. This has been the aim of this book. In this Postscript, I return to some areas that offer promise but may not yet be fully exploited.

Are We Taking Sufficient Account of Carryover Effects?

Some campaigns are dramatically better than others. For example, the Wonderbra campaign in which Eva Herzigova featured generated an enormous return, given the low cost of the campaign. The ads themselves were genuinely creative and resulted in a massive amount of consequential interest and comment. Part of this comment was via the media but there was clearly substantial word of mouth, which helped to popularize the product. It is not my purpose here to explain how to be creative, but it is useful to show how creativity can produce results. In this case, the carryover effects made the campaign much more effective.

Carryover effects are not measured directly in ad tests. Fortunately, we know that primary effects are required for carryover effects, so a test for a primary effect is a start. But not all the ads that produce a primary effect produce a carryover effect. This may be because competitor advertising nullifies any later effect of a campaign, but it also seems likely that some ads for some products have more potential to develop carryover effects. This is an area where we need more research so that we can predict carryover success. We should look again at the way ads are tested and campaigns are constructed to see whether they possess the potential to create comment, recommendation, emulation and increased distribution. It is particularly important to stimulate word of mouth since this has so much impact on the take-up of many products, particularly services. Here, print and Internet media may provide a supportive role by providing material that people are happy to repeat to others.

A further thought on carryover effects is that we need to know how such effects are changed when the benefit of advertising is taken as a margin increase rather than as a sales lift. It seems likely that a margin increase would reduce carryover effects, but research is needed on this matter.

Do We Change Copy Often Enough?

The decision to change copy may be deferred too long as Lodish and Lubetkin (1992) pointed out. There are two particular constraints here. One is the understandable reluctance on the part of creative staff to see their ideas discarded and the second is cost, particularly the cost of TV commercials. One of the advantages of *not* using television is that a larger set of options can be generated at a more modest cost.

A problem here is a lack of understanding of copy wearout. One approach is to treat wearout as an empirical matter, testing each prospective copy introduction against current advertising. In the United States, IRI encourages advertisers to use their test communities to evaluate potential changes in copy and scheduling. If the evaluations give positive results they can be implemented nationally. This can be done less precisely by trying out new ads in a TV area and or a local newspaper.

But we need a theory that explains wearout. What exactly is wearing out? The model presented in Chapter 3 proposed that ads have two primary effects. One effect was confined to the first few exposures and involved some thoughtful appraisal of ad content; this process could produce quite substantial changes in the behavior of an audience but happened only once for an ad if it occurred at all. The other primary effect rested on automatic mechanisms that strengthened the brand's salience, value and associations; this could persist over quite a large number of ad repetitions. This model needs more testing. It suggests that ads can take many exposures to wear out but that it may still be worth bringing forward new copy early if that copy is not too expensive to produce and is effective in eliciting a thoughtful response.

Using Evidence on the Durability and Decay of Advertising?

One explanation for the decay in sales effect is that it occurs as a result of interference from competitor advertising. One implication of this cause of decay is that ads should be presented as soon as possible after competitor exposures so that any loss of salience for a brand is countered as quickly as possible. But schedules for advertising are not easily specified against the contingencies of competitive advertising. A second implication is that some brands will benefit more from advertising because they have not been advertised for some time, and competitors have gained ascendancy.

Recent research shows that long-term decay is usually quite slow so that the effect from ad exposures can last for years. When the financial return from advertising is properly assessed and takes account of this long-lasting effect, campaigns are seen to bring more benefit than has been previously thought.

The long-term effect of advertising also has a bearing on the way in which ad agencies are paid. The common methods that have been used are commission on ad expenditure, fee, and payment by results. It is difficult to justify commission payment. The effectiveness of different campaigns varies too much. Surely, those who developed the Stella Artois campaigns deserve more than those who produced the less successful but more costly campaigns for rival beers. Similarly, it is difficult to justify a fee system that is not linked to results. The last option, payment by results, depends on measurement of effectiveness and this could be highly contentious. Long-term effect is substantial but cannot be assessed within a reasonable time frame and probably reflects the vagaries of competitor advertising as much as the strength of copy for the focal brand. There is clearly no easy solution here but payment on short-term effect seems realistic, given that the evidence shows that this is required for any long-term effect to occur.

Short-term decay may also be exploited where purchasing varies by day of the week. We saw from Roberts' work that short-term decay was so rapid that ads for groceries on Wednesday or Thursday were likely to have substantially more effect on sales than the same ads on Saturday or Sunday.

How Should We Use Different Media?

In Southern European countries (such as Italy and Greece) and in the United States, television is the biggest advertising medium by expenditure but, in many other countries, it is print that dominates. TV advertising is usually very expensive and this raises interest in other media, such a radio, magazines, the Internet and billboard.

The different media have different effects on recall and recognition. If brand recognition is required, as in grocery markets, television serves well. Magazine and billboards also excel here. Radio can provide audio recognition for products such as popular music but, otherwise, it is better for recall. This means that many services do well with radio advertising because services are usually bought on the basis of recall.

Multi-media plans are becoming more popular and rest in part on evidence that they make more effective use of the adspend but there is a problem in interpreting such evidence. As more media are used, more ad copy versions are produced, so that the sales gains that are observed might be due partly to reduced wearout. It is possible that the gains found in some studies could have been achieved with television alone if the copy used had been more varied and the media plan adjusted to increase penetration.

Are We Using The Power of Display Effectively?

Display and other features of the purchase context serve to revive the ad message in the mind of the customer at the point where purchase can take place. It is important, therefore, to forge links between the ad and the purchase context.

Signals at the point of sale can induce immediate purchase. We can observe this in the retail context fairly clearly. Purchases of a discounted Sauvignon wine may be several times those for the same wine when it is not discounted. The effect is partly due to price but is also attributable to the way the price reduction is communicated by notice and product display. This suggests that we need to understand better how point-of-sale material works so that we can improve its design. Manufacturers have a rather tenuous control on display in the store and may need to develop more cooperation with retailers.

What Is the Potential of Internet Advertising?

It is clear that ads on the Internet can build brand awareness and so influence purchases made through conventional outlets. Despite the failure of many specialist Internet companies, there is substantial growth in Internet purchasing as more people start to buy more categories in this way. The Internet may particularly favor niche products because advertising can be associated with relevant fields defined by directories or search engines. One study of the air carrier, EasyJet, exhibited widely different response rates from different websites and this indicates the importance of targeting in this medium. However, many products with broader appeal have less use for such precision delivery of advertising.

Do We Target the Right Loyalty Segments?

Customer-based marketing has led to a focus on retaining customers in segments defined by their levels of loyalty and usage. Some reassessment of this emphasis may be required. It appears that the focus on existing customers could, in the end, reduce the recruitment of new customers. This emerges when we look at how media advertising affects the different loyalty segments. More extra volume *per customer* comes via advertising to the *fairly* loyal but the number of customers in the low-loyalty segment is very large and this means that there is usually more total sales gain from advertising *to this segment*. Databases omit non-customers and under-enroll low-loyalty customers so that media advertising is required to make good contact with consumers who have little or no loyalty. In this way, media advertising does a different job when compared with direct marketing. Direct marketing often has costs that are based on customer contact and, when this applies, it should focus on those customers with higher loyalty who are likely to show more individual volume gain. Media advertising is the more effective channel to the low-loyalty customer, of whom some may become stronger customers. This analysis indicates that media advertising and database marketing are complementary rather than alternative strategies.

Advertising Terms

Opportunities-to-see (OTS) or **exposures** are the occasions when people see the ad (or could see it because the TV is on). These may be expressed as a **frequency** for a period, e.g. three exposures in a 28-day period. Print and some Internet advertising are charged for on the basis of cost per thousand impressions (or exposures).

Reach or **coverage** is a measure of advertising penetration. It is the proportion of a target population exposed to the ad at least once in a time period.

Television rating (TVR) is the percentage of the potential TV audience exposed to an ad or campaign. The sum of the TVRs for each showing of the commercial is a measure of total advertising weight. In the United States, this sum is called gross rating points (GRPs)

Advertising weight is an amount of advertising, measured by TVR/GRP or by spend. An **upweight** is an increase in advertising weight in a period.

Weight tests measure the impact of an upweight on sales.

Copy tests evaluate the effect of an ad on sales or on measures that are claimed to relate to sales.

The schedule specifies whether ads are aired in short blocks (pulses), longer blocks, (bursts) or more continuously. The schedule affects frequency and reach.

The media plan specifics the frequency, reach, and continuity objectives to be secured by the use of specified media over a time period.

A campaign may use a number of different ad executions and more than one medium.

Advertising elasticity is usually measured as the proportionate increase in sales divided by the proportionate increase in advertising. This assumes that the brand price and the ad costs are unchanging.

Useful Websites

Attention is drawn to the following websites:

www.ipa.co.uk carries a complete listing of cases in the IPA data bank, plus other useful information.

www.warc.com is the website for the World Advertising Research Center and carries information on research, case histories and current activities.

www.adforum.com shows creative work.

www.arfsite.org is the Advertising Research Foundation's website.

References

Abraham, M.M. and Lodish, L.M. (1990) Getting the most out of advertising and promotion, *Harvard Business Review*, 68, 3, 50-60.

Adams, H.F. (1916) *Advertising and its Mental Laws*, New York, Macmillan.

Ahluwalia, R., Burnkrant R.E., and Unnava H.R. (2000) Consumer response to negative publicity, *Journal of Marketing Research*, 37, May, 203-214.

Ajzen, I. and Fishbein, M. (1977) Attitude-behavior relations: a theoretical analysis and review of empirical research, *Psychological Bulletin*, 84, 888-918.

Ambler, T. and Broadbent, S. (2000) A dialogue on advertising effectiveness and efficiency, *Admap*, July/August, 29-31.

Ambler, T. and Burne, T. (1999) The impact of affect on memory, *Journal of Advertising Research*, 39, 2, 25-34.

ARF (2000) www.arfsite.org/Webpages/informed/april2000/page5.html

Baker, C. (1993) *Advertising Works 7*, Henley-on-Thames, Institute of Practitioners in Advertising, NTC Publications.

Baker, C. (1995) *Advertising Works 8*, Henley-on-Thames, Institute of Practitioners in Advertising, NTC Publications.

Baldinger, A.L. and Rubinson, J. (1996) Brand loyalty: the link between attitude and behavior, *Journal of Advertising Research*, Nov/Dec, 22-34.

Baldinger, A.L. and Rubinson, J. (1997) In search of the Holy Grail: a rejoinder, *Journal of Advertising Research*, 36, 6, 18-20.

Baldwin, M.W. and Holmes, J.G. (1987) Salient private audiences and awareness of the self, *Journal of Personality and Social Psychology*, 52, 1087-1098.

Barnard, N. and Ehrenberg, A. (1997) Advertising: strongly persuasive or nudging? *Journal of Advertising Research*, 37, 1, 21-31.

Bass, F.M. (1969) A new product growth model for consumer durables, *Management Science*, 15, 1, 215-227.

Batra, R. and Ray, M.L. (1983) Advertising situations: the implications of differential involvement and accompanying affect responses. In Harris, R.L. (Ed.) *Information Processing Research in Advertising*, London, Lawrence Erlbaum Associates, 127-51.

Bayus, B.L. (1991) The consumer durable replacement buyer, *Journal of Marketing*, 55, January, 42-51.

Berlyne, D.E. (1954) A theory of human curiosity, *British Journal of Psychology*, 45, 180-191.

Blair, M.H. (1987) An empirical investigation of advertising wearin and wearout, *Journal of Advertising Research*, 27, 6, 45-50.

Blair, M.H. and Rabuck, M.J. (1998) Advertising wearin and wearout: ten years later – more empirical evidence and successful practice, *Journal of Advertising Research*, October, 7-17.

Bolton, R.N. (1989) The relationship between market characteristics and promotional price elasticities, *Marketing Science*, 8, 2, 153-169.

Bornstein, R.F. (1989) Exposure and affect: overview and meta-analysis of research, *Psychological Bulletin*, 106, 2, 265-89.

Braun, K.A. (1999) Postexperience advertising effects on consumer memory, *Journal of Consumer Research*, 25, March, 319-334.

Brehm, J.W. and Cohen, A.R. (1962) *Explorations in Cognitive Dissonance*, New York, Wiley.

Briesch, R.A., Lakshman, K., Tridib, M., and Raj, S.P. (1997) A comparative analysis of reference price models, *Journal of Consumer Research*, 24, September, 202-214.

Broadbent, S. (1984) Modelling with adstock, *Journal of the Market Research Society*, 26, 4, 295-312.

Broadbent, S. (1989) *The Advertising Budget: The Advertiser's Guide to Budget Determination*, Henley, NTC Publications.

Broadbent, S. (1995) Single source - the breakthrough? *Admap*, June, 29-33.

Broadbent, S. (1998) Effective frequency: there and back, *Admap*, May, 34-38.

Broadbent, S. and Colman, S. (1986) Advertising effectiveness: across brands, *Journal of the Market Research Society*, 28, 1, 15-24.

Broadbent, S. and Fry, T. (1995) Adstock modelling for the long term, *Journal of the Market Research Society,* 37, 4, 385-403.

Broadbent, S., Spittler, J.Z., and Lynch, K. (1997) Building better TV schedules: new light from the single source, *Journal of Advertising Research*, 37, 4, 27-31.

Broadbent, T. (1999) What's the use of tracking studies? *Admap*, November, 18-20.

Broadbent, T. (2000) *Advertising Works 11*, IPA, WARC, Henley-on-Thames.

Brown, G. (1986) Monitoring advertising performance, *Admap*, 22, 3, 151-53.

Brown, G. (1991) *How Advertising Affects the Sales of Packaged Goods Brands: a Working Hypothesis for the 1990s*, Millward Brown International plc.

Brown, J.J. and Reingen, P.H. (1987) Social ties and word-of-mouth referral behavior, *Journal of Consumer Research*, 14, December, 350-362.

Bullmore, J. (1998) *Behind the Scenes in Advertising*, Henley-on-Thames, Admap Publications, 115-130.

Burke, R.R. and Srull, T.K. (1988) Competitive interference and consumer memory for advertising, *Journal of Consumer Research*, 15, June, 55-68.

Burnkrant, R.E. and Unnava, H.R. (1987) Effects of variation in message execution on the learning of repeated brand information. In Wallendorf, M. and Anderson, P. (Eds.) *Advances in Consumer Research*, 14, 173-76.

Cacioppo, J.T. and Petty, R.E. (1979a) Attitudes and cognitive response: an electrophysiological approach, *Journal of Personality and Social Psychology,* 37, 2181-2199.

Cacioppo, J.T. and Petty, R.E. (1979b) Effects of message repetition and position on cognitive response, recall and persuasion, *Journal of Personality and Social Psychology,* 37, 97-109.

Cacioppo, J.T. and Petty, R.E. (1985) Central and peripheral routes to persuasion: the role of message repetition. In L.F. Alwitt and A.A. Mitchell (Eds.) *Psychological Processes and Advertising Effects*, Hillsdale, N.J., Erlbaum, 91-111.

Chaiken, S., Liberman, A., and Eagly, A.H. (1989) Heuristic and systematic information processing within and beyond the persuasion context. In J.S. Uleman and J.A. Bargh (Eds.) *Unintended Thought*, New York, Guildford Press, 212-252.

Channon, C. (1985) *Advertising Works 3*, London, Holt, Rinehart and Winston.

Clarke, D.G. (1976) Econometric measurement of the duration of advertising effect on sales, *Journal of Marketing Research* 13, 4, 345-57.

Colley, R.H. (1961) *Defining Advertising Goals and Measuring Advertising Results*, New York, Association of National Advertisers.

Confer, M.G. (1992) The media multiplier: nine studies conducted in seven countries, *Journal of Advertising Research*, 32, 1, RC4-RC10.

Dall 'Olmo Riley, F., Ehrenberg, A.S.C., Castleberry, S.B., Barwise, T.P., and Barnard, N.R. (1997) The variability of attitudinal repeat-rates, *International Journal of Research in Marketing*, 14, 5, 437-450.

Danaher, P.J. and Brodie, R.J. (2000) Understanding the characteristics of price elasticities for frequently purchased packaged goods, *Journal of Marketing Management,* 16, 8, 917-936.

Deighton, J. (1984) The interaction of advertising and evidence, *Journal of Consumer Research*, 11, December, 763-770.

Dickson, P.R. and Sawyer, A.G. (1990) The price knowledge and search of supermarket shoppers, *Journal of Marketing*, 54, July, 42-53.

Donovan, R.J., Rossiter, J.R., Marcoolyn, G., and Nesdale A. (1994) Store atmosphere and purchasing behavior, *Journal of Retailing*, 70, 3, 283-94.

Duckworth, G. (1997) *Advertising Works 9*, NTC Publications, Henley-on-Thames.

Eagly, A.H. and Chaiken, S. (1993) *The Psychology of Attitudes*, Orlando, Harcourt Brace Jovanovitch.

East, R. and Hammond, K.A. (1996) The erosion of repeat-purchase loyalty, *Marketing Letters*, 7, 2, 163-72.

East, R. and Lomax, W. (2002) Recommendation as a function of customer tenure, ANZMAC, Melbourne.

East, R., Williamson, M., and Eftichiadou, V. (2003) Point-of-purchase display and brand sales. *International Review of Retail, Distribution and Consumer Research*, 13, 1, 127-134.

Effective Advertising 5 (2000) Advertising Federation of Australia, South Yarra, Victoria, Hardie Grant Books.

Effective Advertising 6 (2001) Advertising Federation of Australia, South Yarra, Victoria, Hardie Grant Books.

Ehrenberg, A.S.C. (1974) Repetitive advertising and the consumer, *Journal of Advertising Research*, 14, 2, 25-34.

Ehrenberg, A.S.C. (1988) *Repeat Buying: Theory and Applications*, 2nd Edition, London, Charles Griffin & Co. (first published in 1972 by North Holland).

Ehrenberg, A.S.C. (1997) In search of Holy Grails: two comments, *Journal of Advertising Research*, 37, 1, 9-12.

Ehrenberg, A.S.C., Hammond, K.A., and Goodhardt, G.J. (1994) The after-effects of price-related consumer promotions, *Journal of Advertising Research,* 34, 4, 11-21.

Ehrenberg, A.S.C. and Pouilleau, B. (1991) The pattern of car switching. Unpublished working paper.

Engage (2001) www.engage.com/uk/press_room/viewpress.cfm?urlcode=022101carat

Farris, P.W. and Albion, M.S. (1980) The impact of advertising on the price of consumer goods, *Journal of Marketing*, 44, 3, 17-35.

Farris, P.W. and Reibstein, D.J. (1979) How prices, ad expenditures, and profits are linked, *Harvard Business Review*, 57, 6, 173-84.

Fazio, R.H. (1986) How do attitudes guide behavior? In Sorrentino, R.M. and Higgins, E.T. (Eds.) *The Handbook of Motivation and Cognition: Foundations of Social Behavior*, New York, Guildford Press.

Fazio, R.H. (1990) Multiple processes by which attitudes guide behavior: the mode model as an integrative framework. In Zanna, M.P. (Ed.) *Advances in Experimental Social Psychology*, 23, 75-109.

Fazio, R.H., Powell, M.C., and Herr, P.M. (1983) Toward a process model of the attitude-behavior relation: Accessing one's attitude upon mere observation of the attitude object, *Journal of Personality and Social Psychology*, 44, 723-35.

Fazio, R.H. and Zanna, M.P. (1981) Direct experience and attitude-behavior consistency. In Berkowitz, L. (Ed.) *Advances in Experimental Social Psychology*, 14, New York, Academic Press.

Feldwick, P., (1990) *Advertising Works 5*, Henley-on-Thames, Institute of Practitioners in Advertising, NTC Publications.

Feldwick, P., (1991) *Advertising Works 6*, Henley-on-Thames, Institute of Practitioners in Advertising, NTC Publications Ltd.

Festinger, L. and Maccoby, N., (1964) On resistance to persuasive communications, *Journal of Abnormal and Social Psychology*, 58, 203-210.

Fiske, S.T. (1980) Attention and weight in person perception: the impact of negative and extreme behavior, *Journal of Personality and Social Psychology,* 38, 6, 889-906.

Fiske, S.T. and Taylor, S.E. (1991) *Social Cognition*, 2nd Edition, New York, McGraw-Hill.

Flores, L (2000) Internet advertising effectiveness: what did we learn and where are we going. Worldwide Advertising Conference, Rio de Janiero, November (LFlores@ipsos-asi.com).

Flores, L. (2001) Ten things you should know about online advertising, *Admap*, April, 34-35.

Francolini, M. (1999) *Profitability Through Customers: Why Retention is the Answer*, BA Dissertation, Kingston University.

Franzen, G. (1994) *Advertising Effectiveness*, Henley-on-Thames, NTC Publications.

Fulgoni, G.M. (1987) The role of advertising - is there one? *Admap*, April, 54-7.

Gabor, A. and Granger, C.W.J. (1961) On the price consciousness of consumers, *Applied Statistics*, 10, 3, 170-88.

Gardner, M.P. (1985) Mood states and consumer behavior: a critical review, *Journal of Consumer Research*, 12, December, 281-300.

Gatignon, H. and Robertson, T.S. (1985) A propositional inventory for new diffusion research, *Journal of Consumer Research*, 11, March, 849-867.

Gatignon, H. and Robertson, T. S. (1991) Innovative decision processes. In Robertson, Thomas S. and Kassarjian, Harold H. (Eds.) *Handbook of Consumer Behavior*, Englewood Cliffs, New Jersey, Prentice Hall, 316-348.

Givon, M. and Horsky, D. (1990) Untangling the effects of purchase reinforcement and advertising carryover, *Marketing Science*, 9, 2, 171-87.

Gladwell, M. (2000) *The Tipping Point*, Boston, Little Brown & Co.

Guadagni, P.M. and Little, J.D.C. (1983) A logit model of brand choice calibrated on scanner data, *Marketing Science*, 2, Summer, 203-38.

Guido, G. (2001) *The Salience of Marketing Stimuli: An Incongruity-Salience Hypothesis on Consumer Awareness*, Dordrecht, Kluwer Academic Press.

Gutman, J. (1982) A means-end chain model based on consumer categorization processes, *Journal of Marketing*, 46, 2, 60-72.

Haley, R.I. and Baldinger, A.L. (1991) The ARF copy research validation project, *Journal of Advertising Research*, April-May, 11-32.

Hamilton, W., East, R., and Kalafatis, S. (1997) The measurement and utility of brand price elasticities, *Journal of Marketing Management*, 13, 4.

Hanssens, D.M., Parsons, L.J., and Schultz, R.L. (2001) *Market Response Models: Econometric and Time Series Analysis*, 2nd Edition, Dordrecht, Netherlands, Kluwer Academic Publishers.

Heath, R. (2000a) Low involvement processing Part 1: a neuroscientific explanation of how brands work, *Admap*, March, 14-16.

Heath, R. (2000b) Low involvement processing Part 2: seven new rules for evaluating brands and their communication, *Admap*, April, 34-36.

Heath, R. (2001) *The Hidden Power of Advertising: How Low Involvement Processing Influences the Way We Choose Brands*, Henley-on-Thames, Admap Publications.

Hoffman, D.L. and Novak, T. (2000) How to acquire customers on the Web, *Harvard Business Review*, May-June, 179-188.

Holden, S.J.S. and Lutz, R.J. (1992) Ask not what the brand can evoke; ask what can evoke the brand. In Sherry, J.F. and Sternthal, B. (Eds.) *Advances in Consumer Research*, 19, 101-107.

Ingram, A. and Cory, P. (2001) An insight into radio advertising effectiveness, *Admap*, March, 44-48.

IRI (1989) Larger sample, stronger proof of P-O-P effectiveness. Reprint from IRI which enlarges on a report that first appeared in *P-O-P Times*, March/April, 28-32, 1989.

Janiszewski, C. (1988) Preconscious processing effects: the independence of attitude formation and conscious thought, *Journal of Consumer Behavior*, 15, September, 199-209.

Johnson, B.T. and Eagly, A.H. (1989) The effects of involvement on persuasion: a meta-analysis, *Psychological Bulletin*, 106, 290-314.

Jones, J.P. (1995a) *When Ads Work: New Proof That Advertising Triggers Sales*. New York, Lexington Books.

Jones, J.P. (1995b) Single source research begins to fulfill its promise. *Journal of Advertising Research*, 35, 3, 9-16.

Jones, J.P. (1995c) Advertising exposure effects under a microscope, *Admap*, February, 28-31.

Jones, J.P. (1995d) We have a breakthrough, *Admap*, June, 33-5.

Jones, J.P. (1998) Point of view: STAS and BehaviorScan – yet another view, *Journal of Advertising Research*, March/April, 51-53.

Jones, J.P. and Blair, M.H. (1996) Examining "conventional wisdoms" about advertising effects with evidence from independent sources, *Journal of Advertising Research*, November/December, 37-59.

Kaul, A. and Wittink, D.R. (1995) Empirical generalizations about the impact of advertising on price sensitivity and price, *Marketing Science*, 14, 3, Part 2 of 2, G151-G160.

Keaveney, S.M. (1995) Customer switching behavior in service industries: an exploratory study, *Journal of Marketing*, 59, 71-82.

Kendall, N. (1998) *Advertising Works 10*, Henley-on-Thames, NTC Publications.

Kroloff, G. (1988) At home and abroad: weighing in, *Public Relations Journal*, 44, October, 8.

Krugman, H.E. (1972) Why three exposures may be enough, *Journal of Advertising Research*, 12, 6, 11-14.

Lannon, J. and Cooper P. (1983) Humanistic advertising: a holistic cultural perspective, *International Journal of Advertising*, 2, 195-213.

Lattin, J.M. and Bucklin, R.E. (1989) Reference effects of price and promotion on brand choice behavior, *Journal of Marketing Research*, 26, August, 299-310.

Lau, G.T. and Ng, S. (2001) Individual and situational factors influencing negative word-of-mouth behaviour. *Canadian Journal of Administrative Sciences*, 18, 3, 163-178.

Lavidge, R.J. and Steiner, G.A. (1961) A model for predictive measurements of advertising effectiveness, *Journal of Marketing*, 25, October, 59-62.

Lazarsfeld, P.F. (1944) *The People's Choice*, New York, Duell, Sloan and Pearce.

Leckenby, J.D. and Kim, H. (1994) How media directors view reach/frequency, *Journal of Advertising Research*, 34, September/October, 9-21.

Leone, R.P. (1995) Generalizing what is known about temporal aggregation and advertising carryover, *Marketing Science*, 14, 3 (2), G141-G150.

Litzenroth, H. (1991) A small town in Germany: single source data from a controlled micromarket, *Admap*, 26, 5, 23-27.

Lodish, L.M. (1997) Point of view: J.P. Jones and M.H. Blair on measuring advertising effects – another point of view, *Journal of Advertising Research*, September/October, 75-79.

Lodish, L.M. (1998) STAS and BehaviorScan – it's not that simple, *Journal of Advertising Research*, March/April, 54-56.

Lodish, L.M., Abraham, M., Kalmansen, S., Livelsberger, J., Lubetkin, B., Richardson, B., and Stevens, M.E. (1995a) How T.V. advertising works: a meta-analysis of 389 real world split cable T.V. advertising experiments, *Journal of Marketing Research*, 32, 2, 125-39.

Lodish, L.M., Abraham, M., Livelsberger, J., Lubetkin, B., Richardson, B., and Stevens, M.E. (1995b) The long-term effect of TV advertising, *Marketing Science*, 14, 3 (2), G133-G140.

Lodish, L.M. and Lubetkin, B. (1992) How advertising works. General truths? Nine key findings from IRI test data, *Admap*, February, 9-15.

McDonald, C. (1970) What is the short-term effect of advertising? *Proceedings of the ESOMAR Congress*, Barcelona, 463-85.

McDonald, C. (1992) *How Advertising Works*, Henley-on-Thames, The Advertising Association and NTC Publications.

McDonald, C. (1995a) *Advertising Reach and Frequency*, Chicago, NTC Business Books.

McDonald, C. (1995b) Where to look for the most trustworthy evidence. Short-term advertising effects are the key, *Admap*, Feb, 25-7.

McDonald, C. (1995c) Breakthrough or bun fight, *Admap*, June, 35-8.

McGuire, W.J. (1968) Personality and attitude change: an information processing theory. In A.G. Greenwald, T.C. Brock and T.M Ostrom (Eds.) *Psychological Foundations of Attitudes*, 171-196, San Diego, California, Academic Press.

Madden, T.J. and Ajzen, I. (1991) Affective cues in persuasion: an assessment of causal mediation, *Marketing Letters*, 2, 4, 359-366.

Mahajan, V., Muller, E., and Bass, F. (1990) New product diffusion models in marketing: a review and directions for research, *Journal of Marketing*, 54, January, 1-26.

Malec, J. (1982) Ad testing through the marriage of UPC scanning and targetable TV, *Admap*, May, 273-279.

Mangold, W.G., Miller, F., and Brockway, G.R. (1999) Word-of-mouth communication in the service marketplace, *Journal of Services Marketing*, 13, 1, 73-89.

Mela, C.F., Gupta, S. and Lehmann, D.R. (1997) The long-term impact of promotion and advertising on consumer choice, *Journal of Marketing Research*, 34, May, 248-261.

Milliman, R.E. (1982) Using background music to affect the behavior of supermarket shoppers, *Journal of Marketing*, 46, Summer, 86-91.

Mizerski, R.W. (1982) An attributional explanation of the disproportionate influence of unfavorable information, *Journal of Consumer Research*, 9, 1, 301-310.

Moldovan, S.E. (1984) Copy factors related to persuasion scores, *Journal of Advertising Research*, 24, 6, 16-22.

Moraleda, P. and Ferrer-Vidal, J. (1991) Proceedings of the 1990 ESOMAR Conference, Monte Carlo.

Naik, P.A. (1999) Estimating the half-life of advertising, *Marketing Letters*, 10, 3, 351-362.

Naples, M.J. (1979) *Effective Frequency: The Relationship Between Frequency and Advertising Effectiveness*, New York, Association of National Advertisers.

Nielsen (2003) *The British Shopper*, Headington, Oxford, NTC Publications.

North, A.C., Hargreaves, D.J., and McKendrick, J. (1997) In-store music affects product choice, *Nature*, 390, November, 132.

Osterhouse, R.A. and Brock, T.C. (1970) Distracting increases yielding to propaganda by inhibiting counterarguing, *Journal of Personality and Social Psychology*, 15, 344-358.

Pearce, L., (2000) *Loyalty as a Function of the Duration of Brand Ownership*. MA dissertation, Kingston University.

Pechmann, C. and Stewart, D.W. (1988) Advertising repetition: a critical review of wearin and wearout. In *Current Issues and Research in Advertising*, 11, 2, 285-329.

Petty, R.E. and Cacioppo, J.T. (1985) The elaboration likelihood model of persuasion. In Berkowitz, L. (Ed.) *Advances in Experimental Social Psychology*, 19, New York, Academic Press.

Petty, R.E. and Cacioppo, J.T. (1986a) *Communication and Persuasion: Central and Peripheral Routes to Attitude Change*, New York, Springer-Verlag.

Petty, R.E. and Cacioppo, J.T. (1986b) An elaboration likelihood model of persuasion. In L. Berkowitz, (Ed.) *Advances in Experimental Social Psychology*, 19, 123-205, New York, Academic Press.

Petty, R.E., Wells, G.L., and Brock, T.C. (1976) Distraction can enhance or reduce yielding to propaganda: thought disruption versus effort justification, *Journal of Personality and Social Psychology*, 34, 874-884.

Plessis, E. du (1994) Understanding and using likability, *Journal of Advertising Research*, 34, September/October, RC3-RC10.

Plessis, E. du (1998) Advertising likeability, *Admap*, October, 34-36.

Pomerance, E. and Zielske, H. (1958) How frequently should you advertise? *Media/Scope*, 2, 9, 25-7.

Raj, S.P. (1982) The effects of advertising on high and low loyalty segments, *Journal of Advertising Research*, 9, June, 77-89.

Reichheld, F.F. and Schefter, P. (2000) E-loyalty: your secret weapon on the Web, *Harvard Business Review*, July/August, 105-113.

Rice, B. and Bennett, R. (1998) The relationship between brand usage and advertising tracking measurements: international findings, *Journal of Advertising Research*, 38, 3, 58-66.

Rimini, M. (2003) Advertising Works 12, Henley-on-Thames, IPA and WARC.

Riskey, D.R. (1997) How TV advertising works: an industry response, *Journal of Market Research*, 34, May, 292-293.

Roberts, A. (1996) What do we know about advertising's short-term effects? *Admap*, February, 42-45.

Roberts, A. (1998) Measuring the short-term sales effects of TV advertising, *Admap*, April, 50-52.

Roberts, A. (1999) Recency, frequency and the sales effects of TV advertising, *Admap*, February, 40-44.

Roberts, A. (2000) tvSpan: the medium-term effects of TV advertising, *Admap*, November, 12-14.

Rogers, E.M. (1983) *Diffusion of Innovations*, 3rd Edition, New York, Free Press.

Rosen, D.L. and Olshavsky, R.W. (1987) A protocol analysis of brand choice strategies involving recommendations, *Journal of Consumer Research*, 14, December, 440-444.

Rossiter, J.R. and Percy, L. (1997) *Advertising Communications and Promotion Management*, New York, McGraw-Hill.

Schlosser, A., Shavitt, S., and Kanfer, A. (1999) Internet users' attitudes towards Internet advertising, *Journal of Interactive Marketing*, 13, 3, 34-54.

Schroeder, G., Richardson, B.R., and Sankaralingam, A. (1997) Validating STAS using BehaviorScan, *Journal of Advertising Research*, 37, 4, 33-43.

Scott, D.R. and Solomon, D. (1998) What *is* wearout anyway? *Journal of Advertising Research*, 38, September/October, 19-28.

Scriven, J. (1999) What do we really know about pricing? *Journal of Targeting, Measurement and Analysis for Marketing*, 7, 4, 359-373.

Simon, H., (1979) Dynamics of price elasticity and brand life cycles: an empirical study, *Journal of Marketing Research*, 16, November, 439-452.

Simon, J.L. (1979) What do Zielske's real data show about pulsing? *Journal of Marketing Research*, 16, August, 415-20.

Simon, J.L. and Arndt, J. (1980) The shape of the advertising response function, *Journal of Advertising Research*, 20, 4, 11-28.

Stapel, J. (2000) Advertising effects and their attitudinal background, *Admap,* June, 36-38.

Steiner, R.L. (1973) Does advertising lower consumer prices? *Journal of Marketing*, 37, 4, 19-27.

Steiner, R.L. (1993) The inverse association between the margins of manufacturers and retailers, *Review of Industrial Organisation*, 8, 717-740.

Strong, E.K. (1925) Theories of selling, *Journal of Applied Psychology,* 9, 75-86.

Swinfen-Green, J. (2002a) Can Internet advertising be used for branding? *Admap,* January, 16-19.

Swinfen-Green, J. (2002b) Internet branding 2: media context and value for money, *Admap,* February, 32-35.

Tarde, G. (1903) *The Laws of Imitation*, Translated by Elsie Clews Parsons, New York, Holt.

Tellis, G.J. (1997) Effective frequency: one exposure or three factors, *Journal of Advertising Research,* 37, 4, 75-80.

Tellis, G.J. (1988) Advertising exposure, loyalty and brand purchase: a two-stage model of choice, *Journal of Marketing Research*, 25, May, 134-144.

Vakratsas, D. and Ambler, T. (1999) How advertising works: what do we really know? *Journal of Marketing,* 63, 1, 26-43.

Vanhuele, M. and Drèze, X. (2002) Measuring the price knowledge shoppers bring to the store, *Journal of Marketing*, 66, October, 72-85.

Walling, J., and Owen, S. (2000) Exploring advertising wearout, *Admap,* 35, 2, 20-22.

Wilkie, W.L and Dickson, P.R. (1985) *Shopping For Appliances: Consumers' Strategies and Patterns of Information Search*, Cambridge, Mass., Marketing Science Institute Research Report No 85-108.

Wilson, W.R. and Peterson, R.A. (1989) Some limits on the potency of word-of-mouth information, *Advances in Consumer Research,* 16, 23-29.

Wright, P. (1974) The harassed decision maker: time pressures, distractions and the use of evidence, *Journal of Applied Psychology,* 59, October, 555-561.

Zajonc, R.B. (1968) Attitudinal effects of mere exposure, *Journal of Personality and Social Psychology Monograph Supplement,* 9, 2 Part 2, 1-27.

Zajonc, R.B. and Rajecki, D.W. (1969) Exposure and affect: a field experiment, *Psychonomic Science,* 17, 216-17.

Zeff, R. and Aronson, B. (1999) *Advertising on the Internet,* New York, John Wiley and Sons.

Zielske, H. (1959) The remembering and forgetting of advertising, *Journal of Marketing,* 23, 3, 239-43.

Subject Index

Author Index